Simply, Effectively and Biblically
by Thomas Fusco

©All rights reserved. This book or any portion thereof may not be reproduced or used in any manner whatsoever without the express written permission of the publisher except for the use of brief quotations in a book review.

Print ISBN: 978-1-54398-782-9

eBook ISBN: 978-1-54398-783-6

CONTENTS

Dedication 1
Introduction 2
In the Beginning 4
What I Believe! 7
My Conversion on April 3rd 1994 8
Ray Comfort influenced me! 10
Just do it! 18
John MacArthur Personal Evangelism 101 26
Are the Ten Commandments for Today? 31
Hear Ye, Hear Ye, All Rise, Court in Session 34
Tennis Anyone 2005 45
A Suggestion on how NOT to get OFFENDED 51
Japan Mission Trip – January 2008 54
Niagara Falls 71
What happened at a Funeral? 77
Attending other Churches 80
1st Way of the Master Laboratory April 2009 85
Bad day for Tom, Glorious day for the Lord 88
Seminar and Open Air in Tempe 91
One of the Exciting Moments 93
Way of the Master Seminar 95
Way of the Master at Fathers Fellowship 99
Just Another Lunch at Mongolian Barbecue 104
My Surgery, at the Hospital 108
Saturday at Pat's Pizza January 2010 112
Attorney Joe C. Men's Breakfast Meeting 117
Today Honoring the Lord at McDonald's 123
Driving on Bell Rd, a Driver Signaled Me 128

Way of the Master Seminar 131
Husband and Wife take the Good Person Test 135
Stone Age or New Technology 137
Is it TRUE, you just need to BELIEVE? 141
Friday Night at the Art Fair 143
Reaching out to the lost in Tempe AZ. 144
1st Friday Night at the Phoenix Art Fair 146
Wednesday Morning at McDonalds 148
Saturday Night with Tree of Life Church 151
The Phoenix Magazine Knows about us! 153
Our Seed Sower Team in Tempe Saturday 157
Sharing Jesus Christ on ASU Campus 158
1st Friday Night with a man on his knees 160
Catherine's Mom Burial January 2011 161
A Cold Saturday Night in Tempe On Mill Ave. 163
A Night to Glorify the Lord Jesus The Christ 166
A Banner Asking, ARE YOU A GOOD PERSON? 168
1st Friday Night at 3rd and Roosevelt Phoenix 171
Saturday Night with Catherine 173
Saturday Night in Tempe then Taco Bell 178
Comments from Way of The Master Seminar 181
Let Your Light Shine 183
You're going to LOVE this! 185
1st Friday at Phoenix Art Fair 187
Saturday Night on Mill in Tempe Arizona 190
Spenser Taking the Good Person Test 193
Prayer Alone??? 195
1st Friday at the Art Fair 199
180 Movie Project at ASU 203
Friday Night at Phoenix Art Fair 206

Saturday Night on Mill Ave Tempe 209
Please Pray for Amanda 212
Jacob Takes off his Rosary Beards 215
Pray Junior hears the WHOLE TRUTH 218
Way of the Master Seminar with NEW Sowers 220
Saturday Night in Tempe June 2012 223
A night at the Hospital 225
Verses for Marriage Counseling 227
My Testimony Easter Sunday March 2013 236
1st Friday Night at the Phoenix Art Fair 239
1st Friday on 3rd and Roosevelt 241
Thomas Fusco Post from my Blog 245
Saturday Night Live 247
My Birthday at McDonalds PV Mall 250
This Morning's at McDonald's 32nd and Shea 253
Last Night! What a Blessing from the Lord! 256
Reflecting on What Happened at 260
Me at Cigna Out-Patient January 2014 262
This Night was Carter's Night 264
A Tennis Match with Naphtali 266
A Homeless Man with a Heart for God 268
Inmate's 8-year-old daughter prays for Dad 270
Sharing the Gospel at Burger King on Bell Rd. 273
Ever Asked, How Was Your Day? Here's Mine 275
At the Dentist Office 2015 279
My Radio Show, Can You Hear Me Now? 2018 281
Our 23rd Wedding Anniversary 283
Now it's time to say AMEN! 286
Appendix: Links them 287

Dedication

This is dedicated to my wife Catherine, the love of my life since 1995. It's been through her inspiration and continual encouragement that gave me the confidence to make the time so that I should write what the Lord has done for me in my life and how it has affected others.

I would also like to thank some of my brothers in Christ, Keith Ochsner, James Hoffman, David Boring and the youngest one, Brandt Dary, who to me has been the most generous young man I have ever met. Their constant encouraging has prompted me to write this book.

Finally, and the most important, I would like to thank God the creator of Heaven and Earth and His only begotten Son, Jesus the Christ who revealed to me what I must do so that I could be forgiven for all the sins I committed. "REPENT" No longer headed for Hell, but now I have been given the gift of the Holy Spirit who dwells in me, and will be forever in Heaven for eternity!

Introduction

I've heard it said, that the best sermon comes from how you live out your life, well here's mine.

So how does one tell others all about the incredible encounters that life presented because the Lord Jesus Christ through the Holy Spirit indwells within you and you are now Born Again, predestined to do all the good works that He, God, had prepared before-hand? Well as I pondered that question, it dawned on me the answer to that question was coming from my Title,

The Joys of Witnessing Simply Effectively and Biblically

Could I be the vessel that the Lord my God **Could** use? **Would** I be able to be obedient to what information I was about to learn and then have enough courage to share His commands regardless of how it was received? **Should** I then after all that was plainly revealed, apply it in my life as one who now was no longer who I was, but who I had become, a new creation, one who has been adopted into the Kingdom of Heaven. Well, the answer became obvious, through the power of the Holy Spirit,

I did!

What you are about to read are real live encounters that have occurred because of the indwelling of the Holy Spirit. You will be a witness to several encounters that probably would not have happened if the Lord had not revealed His truth to me. Now being embodied with the Holy Spirit to go bodily to proclaim to anyone who crosses my path about what's necessary to obtain eternal life in Heaven. This concept is one that I will ask several times to see how you would proceed when confronted with strangers who cross your path during our short time here on planet Earth.

So, now I would be the one who could simply open the dialogue, rather than as we have been told, to wait till they see your light and they will come to you and ask, "what is it you have that makes you seem different?" This is a lie from Satan! Maybe it may happen but this is not what the Lord requires from us as He stated in Acts 1:8, "I'm leaving, so you can receive the Holy Spirit so that you can be my witness here where you are and then to other places you go to and even the rest of the world." (Paraphrase)

Be careful when you read this, as it might change you!

So, let's get to the point!

This is what happened to me and I gladly share it with you!

In the Beginning

This all started back in April 3rd 1994 when I heard a message from a new Pastor who I only went to hear because the women I wanted to date was going to her church.

She invited me as this would be our 1st date. Little did I know that the God of the Universe was about to open my eyes to the reality of the impending judgement that was already imputed on me, because of the sinful lifestyle that I had been living.

This was not a surprise to me because I was raised Catholic and in my 1st marriage I committed Adultery which led to divorce. Knowing the rules of Catholicism, now I was excommunicated from the Catholic Church. I could no longer go to confession and have the Priest hear about my sins and then give me the prayers to have them wiped away.

Hearing what this man said about anyone who broke God's Laws, His Ten Commandments even just once, was headed for Hell. This was no surprise as I knew that's where I was headed and had no problem with it.

He then stated that if anyone here would stand up and admit they were Law breakers, and if they would place their trust in what Jesus Christ did on the Cross, taking the punishment for the sins they committed, then all the sins would be wiped clean as if they had never happened. Once they did that, they would have a desire, as Jesus proclaimed to Repent and become, Born Again".

So, that morning hearing those words for the first time I knew it was me, he was talking about. I stood up! Interesting enough, the women I was with grabbed my jacket and told me that I didn't have to do it. Broken as I was, I turned to her and stated, "**YES, I DO!**"

Now having received this precious gift of the Holy Spirit, I now began attending Worship on a regular basis in 1994. During the week I attended several men's Bible studies. Now growing in His Word, I came to the realization that I had not been Baptized. I wasn't comfortable giving what they required, "my testimony" in front of several hundred attending Worship.

So, approximately three years later the Baptism was performed in a large bathtub mounted on the wall above the pulpit. That was a scary thought to me and you must remember I was raised Catholic, and was baptized as a baby. I thought that part was already taken care of. But after the Lord opened my eyes to the fact that this was something that I had to do willingly on my own, and not accept that my parents did it for me, I now realized I needed to step up and publicly profess my obedience to Jesus the Christ and be Baptized as He was.

As time marched on my life was no longer only about me. Something happened that I couldn't explain. Now my thoughts and visions were about reading the Bible. The information I was receiving was amazingly fulfilling. The more I gleaned the more I wanted.

Several years had passed when I heard a man on TV give his presentation on how he was able to engage with those, who may be lost by using what seemed to have been eliminated from the teaching from today's pulpit. I myself was satisfied that I was not the one to engage with the lost. My only experience in reaching out was in 1995 with my brother and sister and what a disaster. They, being professing Catholic's, knowing how much they need their Priest to save them. I tried desperately to share with them what I had discovered about what it truly meant to be saved from going to Hell. Just my mentioning that I had accepted Jesus Christ as my Lord and Savior and was now being Born Again, was like a powder keg that would drive them further away.

I was told not to talk like that anymore or I wouldn't be allowed at any of the family events. I knew inside my heart; I couldn't deny Jesus. Even my best friend Bob, who was also raised Catholic, had a problem with me. When I explained to him how I was now Born Again, he took offense to it and stated, "oh so now you think you're better than me, if you want to stay my friend don't bring that up anymore."

So, I'm sure you can see based on my experience in trying to help others come to the Lord, I was not the one who should be doing that. The next several years knowing the response I received from my family and friends, I now realized I didn't have the gift of Evangelism.

For the next two decades, experiencing the rejection and hurt feelings that I received from friends and family, it had motivated me to realize that this was not my gift to share.

But as you read you will see that that has changed!

What I Believe!

I wrote this in my diary on July 12th 2002 @ 5:41am.

I believe that Jesus is whom I want to imitate.

I believe that I if I give my life to Jesus Christ, that I should be baptized in public just like He was, and tell why.

I believe that if I am to grow in my walk with Christ I must have a least one, better to have two, Christian men in my life who can hold me accountable for my words, opinions and actions.

I believe that I should always be ready to obey God and do what would honor him through my thoughts, words and actions.

I believe that if I am harboring anything against anyone, that Jesus requires that I should go to that person, and ask that they forgive me for what I am harboring against them.

I should profess my faith in Jesus Christ to others so that He could use me as conduit to reach others.

(Psalm 19:7, Mark 16:15, Acts 1:8, Acts 10:42
Galatians 3:24, Ephesians 3:20, Ephesians 5:1-21, Philippians 2:13, Colossians 3:1)

My Conversion on April 3rd 1994

I was born into the Roman Catholic faith, and not aware of what a personal relationship with Jesus Christ meant. I just followed the teachings of the priests and attended mass and every week went to confession to have my sins forgiven. I wondered how the priest knew how many Hail Mary's and Our Fathers to say and what gave him the power to forgive my sins?

In 1966, I was excommunicated because of my divorce and could no longer attend mass or receive communion and be forgiven. For the next 28 yrs. I thought I was still a good person, I hadn't killed anyone, but deep down inside I knew I was going to Hell. On April 3rd, 1994 I heard a message, that if I admit to being a sinner and repent, turn from my sins, that I would be forgiven because of what Jesus did for me on the cross. This came as the shock of a lifetime! Let me explain by asking you a couple of questions…

Have you ever lied (even one--fib, white lies, etc.)? Ever stolen (anything--the value is irrelevant)? Jesus said, "Whoever looks upon a woman to lust after her, has committed adultery already with her in his heart." Have you ever looked with lust? If you have said "Yes" to these three questions, by your own admission, you are a lying, thieving, adulterer at heart; and we've only looked at three of the Ten Commandments. What a shock!

God didn't see me as the "good person", that I imagined myself to be… and he doesn't see you that way either. Nothing you've ever done is hid from His Holy Eyes. Will you be innocent or guilty on the Day of Judgment? Listen to your conscience. You know that you will be guilty, and therefore end up in Hell. That's not God's will. He provided a way for you and I to be forgiven.

God sent His Son to take our punishment: "God commended His love toward us, in that, while we were yet sinners, Christ died for us." He was bruised for our iniquities. Jesus then rose from the dead and defeated death.

Your own so-called "goodness" can't get you into heaven any more than mine could. Jesus is the only way to Heaven. He is the "Door," the only "Mediator." There is salvation in no other name, so pray something like this:

"Dear God, I repent of all of my sins (confess them). This day I put my trust in Jesus Christ as my Lord and Savior. Please forgive me and grant me your gift of everlasting life. In the name of Jesus, the Christ I pray, Amen."

My testimony written by Thomas L. Fusco

For more about this go to my website: **www.tillthenetsRFull.org**

Ray Comfort influenced me!

In case you don't know him.

*R*ay **Comfort** (born December 5th 1949) is a New Zealand-born Christian minister and evangelist ...

In 2002, Kirk Cameron joined him and formed an organization *called,* "*The Way of the Master*," with the intention of teaching Christians on how to sharing with the lost. Ray speaks professionally at churches, teaches evangelism seminars, and preaches on the piers at Huntington *Beach*, California.

In 2003 I saw Ray Comfort and Kirk Cameron on a Christian station where they showed the viewers how to go out of their way to reach the lost.

They were at Huntington Beach in California. Ray was on a box with a microphone in his hand asking anyone who passed by if they would like some money, if they could answer some of his trivia question.

He would ask about 2 or 3 trivia questions and then ask if anyone wanted a larger sum of money who could prove to him that they were a GOOD PERSON? WOW! Watching how all who claimed they were, he used four of God's Ten Commandments to show them the were NOT!

After watching till the end, I immediately went to his website, livingwaters.com, and ordered the book *called,* **"God Has a Wonderful Plan for Your Life; The Myth of the Modern Message."** Living Waters Publications 2010.

On pp. 110-112 you can read what Dr. Bill Bright who started Campus Crusade for Christ stated, in his book *Heaven or Hell*. How he never mentioned the word Hell: "I have never felt the need to focus on telling people about Hell." This is how Ray in his book explains their meeting.

"On July 2002, Kirk Cameron and Ray Comfort were invited to Orlando, Florida, to join Dr. Bright at his home for breakfast. After our meal, we sat down in his living room and heard this warm, humble, sincere man of God (then in his eighty-first year) share his heart with us." Let me use his own words from his book *Heaven or Hell*, released that same month, to convey the essence of what he said to us (in all the following excerpts, the emphasis is mine): (pp 110) Because of this information it prompted me to get the book, "Heaven or Hell", written by Dr Bill Bright. Here is what I found starting on section page 32.

"In His approximately 42 months of public ministry, there are 33 recorded instances of Jesus speaking about Hell. No doubt He warned of Hell thousands of times. The Bible refers to Hell a total of 167 times. I wonder with what frequency this eternal subject is found in today's pulpits. *'I confess I have failed in my ministry to declare the reality of Hell as often as I have the love of God and the benefits of a personal relationship with Christ.'*

But Jesus spent more of His time warning His listeners of the impending judgment of Hell than speaking of the joys of heaven. God never planned for any human ever to go to Hell. It has never been my emphasis to focus on Hell because it is a place designed by God for His enemy and his demons.

However, as a result of a steady decline in morals and spiritual vitality in today's culture and a growing indifference to the afterlife, I have come to realize the need for a greater discussion of Hell... I have thus come to see that *'silence, or even benign neglect on these subjects, is disobedience on my part.'* To be silent on the eternal destinations of souls is to be like a sentry failing to warn his fellow soldiers of impending attack. It is like knowing calamity is coming and not sounding the alarm.

By admitting that "*benign neglect on these subjects is disobedience on my part.*" Dr. Bright revealed his honest humility and his genuine love of the truth. He also humbly acknowledged that, by emphasizing God's love and the benefits of coming to Christ, he agreed his approach was not in keeping with Jesus' teaching.

In *Red Sky in the Morning* (published in 1998), after lamenting the rampant hypocrisy among professing believers, Dr. Bright identifies reasons for the problems in the Church. Among the reasons he cites are the fact that many who call themselves Christians really are not, (they are false converts); that many have ignored vital biblical truths about worldliness, sin, and judgment; and that "the pure gospel is not being preached." Instead, Pastors "tread lightly past the fundamentals, handing out a sugarcoated version of faith to men and women whose souls are in eternal jeopardy." He also admits,

"We have misrepresented the Christian life," explaining:

Many preachers mention only the benefits of the Christian life without addressing the necessary disciplines, the trials, and temptations we will endure."

With our culture's emphasis on owning earthly possessions and living the good life, these pastors are fearful of acknowledging the biblical facts about the testing the apostles experienced for their faith. Should we expect anything less in our own lives?

The Bible tells us clearly that all believers will undergo difficulties, trials, and tests. *A belief that Christians are entitled to the "good life" can result in demoralized church members.* Expecting the Christian life to be a bed of roses can be very discouraging to new believers, and to more mature ones as well, when they are jostled by the storms of life. (pp. 217–218)

In the same book, he earnestly pleads with Christians to clean up their lives, then concludes the publication with two pages devoted to the Ten Commandments.

In **Witnessing Without Fear**, Dr. Bright suggests "a careful reading of the New Testament" to determine the method of evangelism "modeled for us throughout Scripture." Please, for the sake of the lost, follow Dr. Bright's advice: examine Scripture to see what Jesus, the disciples, and the early Church did.

Be sure you don't JUST speak about God's love, but also warn the lost about His **wrath** against **sin**, the coming **Day of Judgment**, and the reality of **Hell**. As Dr. Bright himself confessed, to be silent on these subjects was "disobedience on my part." So, to avoid being guilty of "benign neglect," make sure you follow the biblical principles he cited. If you use the "Four Spiritual Laws" approach (Campus Crusade for Christ), simply make four important changes:

1) Be careful not to misrepresent the Christian life by telling sinners that Jesus will improve their lives with a wonderful plan. Don't be like the many preachers who, as Dr. Bright noted, wrongly *"mention only the benefits of the Christian life without addressing the necessary disciplines, the trials, and temptations we will endure."*

2) Avoid the unbiblical mistake of giving the cure of the gospel before you've convinced of the disease of sin. Dr. Bright rightly stated, *"Apart from the deadening effect of the Law, no one would feel the need to cast himself at the mercy of Christ."*

3) Take the time to open up the Ten Commandments to bring the knowledge of sin and lead sinners to Christ. *"Since the time of Moses,"* Dr. Bright wrote, *"the Ten Commandments have shown people their sin and hopelessness and their need for the grace of God in Christ Jesus."*

4) Remember to put in what has been left out. Faithfully include the terrible realities of Judgment Day and Hell. Keep in mind Dr. Bright's admonition: *"Every believer must see this present hour as a God-sent opportunity to warn the lost, of the dangers of hell."*

Most of us tend to look down at the Pharisees with a sense of scorn. It is hard to understand how anyone could prefer their own religious traditions to the Word of the Living God. But if you and I understand the biblical legitimacy of the use of the Law to reach the lost, yet ignore it, and instead preach the traditional modern message, we are no better than them.

However, it is my sincere hope that you see what is at stake, and that you do not prefer the traditions of men above the Word of God. I trust that you are being as the Bereans, and that you are testing what is being said by the standard of the Scriptures… and that you will "hold fast what is good"

(1 Thessalonians 5:21).

So, back to the TV show in 2004, which was called, **"The Way of the Master."** I watched and listened as he commented on how the churches during the turn of the century wanted to find another way to bring people to Christ. What they came up with was, Life Enhancement! Accept Jesus and He'll give you love joy peace and fulfillment. In other words, come to Jesus and have a better life.

WOW! That was an eye opener and not true! I myself lost my family some friends and the business I had owned for several years after the Lord opened my eyes that my sinful lifestyle was leading me to Hell. My life here didn't get better as in worldly terms, but I that know what I had received was better and eternal, what I was experience now was just temporal.

So, further research about this man and his message showed me what the Lord and His writing truly required of those whom He had called. The part that was missing from all the teaching that I had obtained that would give me what the Lord wanted me and others to have, was what was in Psalm 19:7, **"The Law is perfect converting the soul."** Ray showed us how to share with anyone using this Biblical principal by simply asking questions about God's standard, His Ten Commandments.

Could it be that our churches now only wanted to bring outsiders into church, rather than show them their sin so that they could be saved from going to Hell? Even in the New Testament, Paul makes the statement, "That the Law is our schoolmaster to lead us to Christ by faith." Galatians.

3:24. In Romans 7:7, he mentioned that, "He didn't know what sin was, except by the Law."

So, there it was! Ray helped me find out the truth. Ray had showed me that it was the Law that was missing from the Gospel message. Even James 4:6, tells us that, "God is opposed to the proud but gives Grace to the humble."

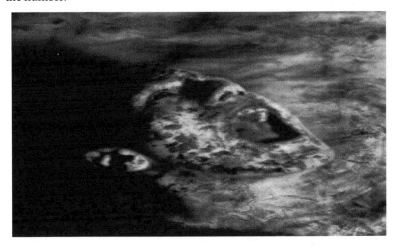

I was convinced! This is real and I'm thankful for hearing the truth about it!

And I'm not going there!

Then I got this from Carl Henderson a missionary in the Philippines
He starts out with, "First, let's understand the "GIFT"
of evangelism. Is it a gift per Ephesians 4:11?"
Ephesians 4:11-12
It was he who gave some to be apostles, some to be prophets, some to be evangelists, and some to be pastors and teachers, to prepare God's people for works of service, so that the body of Christ may be built up.

I believe the so called "five-fold gifts" are better described as functions. If we function in any of them, we become a gift to the church (a blessing) but there is no gift of an Evangelist, Apostle, Prophet, Pastor, or Teacher. They are not so much gifts of individual people but are gifts to the church as the people begin to function successfully in these roles. These people are gifts to the church in that they help to build it up and to equip it.

When I first started out teaching as a newer Christian, people said, "Oh, he has the gift of teaching" and now when we train hundreds of new evangelists every year, they keep on saying, "he is a teacher." However, I was actually taught how to teach adult education in the military and as a Law Enforcement trainer 30 years ago. Although I have continued to improve through the years, it was a learned skill I now use for the Kingdom of God.

Later when I started preaching and a conventional church appointed me as their pastor / minister, people said, "Oh, he has the gift of a pastor and pastoring." Public speaking was also a learned skill from my previous education. Later still, as I mentioned above, when I learned to do evangelism effectively, they said, "He is an evangelist."

In a sense it is all true, but not the way most Christians normally mean it. In fact, you too can be a five-fold minister (some are saying this of me), just get out, get equipped and start functioning in the roles. Some roles are easier to fulfill than others because of our natural bent or temperament.

For instance, pastoring, home visitation, hospital visitations, funerals and counseling were things I dreaded, but as I made myself function in a pastoral role. I have found great joy in the very things I despised. God equips those who are obedient and teachable! I love hospital visitations now because God uses them so powerfully to change lives. Many people come to Christ and begin to participate in church because of hospital visitations and because of the words spoken at funerals. It is a beautiful thing to weep with the heartbroken or share the loss of a loved one with a family you know and love. If we are willing to do what God commands us to do, God's equipping will follow.

Do the job and soon they will say you have the gift of an "Apostle, Prophet, Evangelist, Pastor and Teacher" based on your results and the power of God flowing through you. It is not hard or magic but it is supernatural how God equips those who do the job or function as God commands, i.e., doing the work of an evangelist, pastor, teacher, apostle, or prophet.

So, do I think I have the five-fold gifts? NO! (Not the way people normally think of it.) Do I think I sometimes function in all five areas? YES! Can you do the same? Yes! It may take some time, experience, some mistakes, and maturing along the way, but you can do it! I am still making mistakes but God uses our commitment and availability not our ability or brains.

One more thing... Some use the excuse that they do not have a supernatural, Holy Spirit given "gift" as an excuse to keep from obeying Christ and doing the work of the Kingdom. I believe we could end up answering to God on judgment day for believing and repeating this lie. There are no shortages in the Kingdom of God for those who are faithful, obedient, and available. Get trained and get to work.

Just do it!

*I*s the Way of the Master the only way to witness? Yes and no. No, but in order to be Biblical, witnessing is ALWAYS Law to the proud, grace to the humble.

James 4:6

But he gives us more grace. That is why Scripture says: "God opposes the proud but gives grace to the humble."

1 Peter 5:5

Young men, in the same way be submissive to those who are older. All of you, clothe yourselves with humility toward one another, because, "God opposes the proud but gives grace to the humble."

And I don't know of any other witnessing style that follows the Biblical example, so **YES!**

Now, many people may do great things, helping out underprivileged children, the homeless and hurting. These are good things and we should continue in them, but this is not witnessing. Even if we make it known that we are Christians and that is the reason that we do these things, it still is not sharing the Gospel.

Where is the explanation of what sin is, making it personal instead of some general description of all mankind, so that they can understand their hopeless condition? Where is the description of justice and the obvious consequences of what we deserve? Where is the definition of what repentance really is, and the need do so? Where is the explanation so that we know what we deserve and can completely understand that God would be totally just, totally righteous in His punishment of each and every one of us for eternity?

Only when we understand His holiness, righteousness and justice, and contrast that to our own moral failure and wickedness, can we understand that if justice is served, we would all be in torment for eternity. Only when we know that we deserve that, can we even begin to grasp the concept of His love and what He's done to keep us from what we've all earned by our actions - eternal condemnation. Then we can see that He paid the fine of His own justice for us, that we might be saved from that fate. Then we can see the love and understand that it is not our works that save us, but that our works are done out of gratitude, that they are evidence that we comprehend the great sacrifice made for us out of the great love of God on undeserving, disobedient creatures. Only then does it make sense.

So, let's look into this and see how it works.

A person must understand their need for a Savior (because they've broken God's Law and need to understand it in a personal way), or the Gospel will never make sense to them. For example, if God loves us and has some sort of wonderful plan for our lives, then why would He throw any of us into hell? I mean, if God is all-powerful, and He loves me, I've got nothing to worry about.

I would never throw someone I loved into eternal punishment, so I cannot imagine that God would, either. So then, why would there be any need to change anything in my life? I've got a cosmic insurance policy to keep me out of hell - God loves me and I believe in Him. It would be just plain mean to throw one of His children into hell.

But when we understand that we are not all God's children, we start out as children of wrath and are given the right to be His children through Jesus Christ.

John 1:12
Yet to all who received him, to those who believed in his name, he gave the right to become children of God—

1 John 3:10
This is how we know who the children of God are and who the children of the devil are: Anyone who does not do what is right is not a child of God; nor is anyone who does not love his brother.

Romans 2:5
But because of your stubbornness and your unrepentant heart, you are storing up wrath against yourself for the day of God's wrath, when his righteous judgment will be revealed.

We must understand God's character - holy, righteous and just, in contrast to our own - our hearts are deceitfully wicked, there are none found good, no not one. And yet, (Proverbs 20:6) KJV, says that we will still proclaim our own goodness.

This is why the Law must be given first, with full understanding of how a person has personally broken it. We will not be graded on a curve, we will not be held in contrast to other people, but we will each be held to God's Holy standard, revealed to us in outline form through the Ten Commandments.

The Law is a schoolmaster to lead us to Christ by faith.

Galatians 3:24
So, the law was put in charge to lead us to Christ that we might be justified by faith.

Once one understands how they will stand up to God's holy standard, and can see their own hopeless condition, only then will they come to realize there is nothing they can do to earn God's favor, no possible way they can do anything for themselves. Once they understand that according to God's standard, each and every one of us actually deserves to be thrown into hell for eternity in order for justice to be satisfied, only then can we start to understand the sacrifice made for us. Only then will we begin to comprehend the paying of our fine by God Himself, and then come to Him for salvation, submitting to His authority with gratitude for the undeserved grace and mercy that He has extended to all who will recognize this and give their lives to Him, not trample the sacrifice underfoot to continue the very things that nailed our Savior to the cross.

With that understanding, the Gospel message makes sense, our lives should be different, changed forever, as the fruit of the Spirit manifests in our lives. So, is the Way of the Master the only way to share your faith? Not necessarily. But using the Law then Grace is the only Biblical method to use. As long as you are doing that, you're following the example given in Scripture. I don't think there's any easier way to do this than the way it's explained in the Way of the Master.

Should everyone be preaching on a street corner? Not everyone will do that, but we are commanded to share our faith. We can hand out tracts and speak to people one to one as well as preaching. But we must be doing something.

Many will use the excuse that not everyone is called to be an evangelist. Well, the apostles, prophets, evangelists, pastors and teachers are there to equip believers, to prepare God's people for works of service, so that the body of Christ may be built up, per Ephesians 4:11-12.

The evangelist is the one preaching on the street corner. The evangelist is the one training and equipping people to be obedient and to share their faith with others.

But the evangelist is NOT the only one sharing their faith, for the Great Commission is a command for ALL believers. So how do you share your faith? With whom, and how often? Are you being obedient? The aforementioned are from, Carl Henderson.

Ray Comfort puts it this way:

$\mathcal{D}$o we desire above all things to have a better paying job, a bigger house, thicker carpet, a superior car, and more money? Are we controlled by the lust of the flesh, the lust of the eyes, and the pride of life? Of have we been transformed from the way of this world by "renewing of [our] mind" (Romans 12:2), that we may prove what is that good, and acceptable, and perfect will of God?

Romans 12:2
Do not conform any longer to the pattern of this world, but be transformed by the renewing of your mind. Then you will be able to test and approve what God's will is, his good pleasing and perfect will.

Are our desires now in line with God's desires? Are we above all things "not willing that any should perish, but that all should come to repentance?? (2 Peter 3:9)

2 Peter 3:9
The Lord is not slow in keeping his promise, as some understand slowness. He is patient with you, not wanting anyone to perish, but everyone to come to repentance.

When I get aspirations to do things to reach the unsaved, it is because His desires have become my desires. I can pursue these aspirations, trusting that they are in the will of God, and therefore I can confidently expect Him to grant them. Remember this is not presumption, "an arrogant taking for granted," but a pure, unadulterated desire to do the right thing by reaching out to the lost.

If our covetous heart has been crucified with Christ, our desire won't be for material things, but that none would perish. Scripture actually warns that a covetous prayer will not be answered: "You ask, and receive not, because you ask amiss, that you may consume it upon your lusts." (James 4:3)

James 4:3 When you ask, you do not receive, because you ask with wrong motives, that you may spend what you get on your pleasures.

Instead, if we follow the advice of Psalm 37:4 and delight ourselves in the Lord, the desires of our heart will match His – and those are the desires He will grant.

Psalm 37:4 Delight yourself in the LORD and
He will give you the desires of your heart

So, do our desires line up with God's desires, or are we still thinking of ourselves first? Have we truly been crucified with Him and truly submit to Him as Lord and Savior?

Luke 6:46
"Why do you call me, 'Lord, Lord,' and do not do what I say?

This verse then goes on to give the parable of the wise and foolish builders, and how the destruction was complete for the one who built upon the sand. And here's something interesting. That same parable can be found in the Book of Matthew, directly following the scariest words in the entire Bible, with "therefore."

Matthew 7:21-23
"Not everyone who says to me, 'Lord, Lord,' will enter the kingdom of heaven, but only he who does the will of my Father who is in heaven. Many will say to me on that day, 'Lord, Lord, did we not prophesy in your name, and in your name drive out demons and perform many miracles?' Then I will tell them plainly, 'I never knew you. Away from me, you evildoers!'

Now, these were not even just lukewarm believers. They were doing works in Jesus' Name, but with wrong motivation. How much less might one be known, who is doing nothing?

Back to Luke 6:46. Now I'm Totally Convinced!

Just one more thought about this.

Below is my summary of Paul's writing from 1st Corinthians 2:1-16

Qualifications of an Evangelist

(hint it's NOT of yourself, it's a gift given by the Holy Spirit)

(1st Corinthians 2:1-16)

1. No excellency of speech or wisdom. Just declare what's been seen and heard
2. Not getting sidetracked with unnecessary details. Focus on the Cross
3. Weakness, not trusting in our own strength and ability
4. Must have FEAR (Greek Phobos) that which is caused being scared
5. Must have much trembling: (awareness of our insufficiency)

DO YOU MEET ANY OF THESE QUALIFICATIONS???

Now that you've heard this method my question is, how much training do I need to go to a stranger and ask?

"Did, you get one of these?"

I like would like to leave with this.

Since I accepted Jesus the Christ, I now realize

"I am **NOBODY** telling **EVERYBODY** about **SOMEBODY** who can save **ANYBODY!**"

Would you to be a **NOBODY**?

John MacArthur Personal Evangelism 101

Sharing the Gospel of Jesus Christ Grace to You

Jesus would have failed personal evangelism class in almost every Bible college and seminary I know.

Matthew 19:16-22 describes a young man who looked like the hottest evangelistic prospect the Lord had encountered so far. He was ripe. He was eager. There was no way he would get away without receiving eternal life.

But he did. Instead of getting him to make a decision, in a sense Jesus chased him off. He failed to draw the net. He failed to sign the young man up. Should we allow our ideas of evangelism to indict Jesus? I think we need to allow His example to critique contemporary evangelism. Christ's confrontation of this young man gives us much-needed insight into reaching the lost.

Turmoil of the Heart

Though rich and a ruler while still a young man, he was undoubtedly in turmoil. All his religion and wealth had not given him confidence, peace, joy, or settled hope. There was a restlessness in his soul-an absence of assurance in his heart. He was coming on the basis of a deeply felt need. He knew what was missing: eternal life. His motivation in coming to Christ was faultless.

His attitude was right as well. He wasn't haughty or presumptuous; he seemed to feel his need deeply. There are many people who know they don't have eternal life but don't feel any need for it. Not this young man. He was desperate. There's a sense of urgency in his question, "Teacher, what good thing shall I do that I might have eternal life?" He did not have a prologue; he didn't warm up; he just blurted it out. He even allowed such an outburst in public and risked losing face with all the people who thought he was a spiritual giant already.

A lot of people, in seeking to understand this passage, have taken the young man to task for the question he asked. They say his mistake was in asking "What good thing shall I do?" But he asked a fair question. It wasn't a calculated bid to trap Jesus into condoning self-righteousness. It was a simple, honest question asked by one in search of truth: "What good thing shall I do that I may obtain eternal life?"

The Issue of Sin

But here's where the story takes an extraordinary turn. Jesus' answer to the young man seems preposterous: "If you wish to enter into life, keep the commandments" (v. 17). Strictly speaking, Jesus' answer was correct. If a person kept the law all his life and never violated a single part of it, he would have eternal life. But no one can. Since he had come with the right motive to the right source, asking the right question, why didn't Jesus simply tell him the way of salvation?

Because the young man was missing an important quality. He was utterly lacking a sense of his own sinfulness. His desire for salvation was based on a felt need. He had anxiety and frustration. He wanted joy, love, peace, and hope. But that is an incomplete reason for committing oneself to Christ.

Our Lord didn't offer relief for the rich young ruler's felt need. Instead, he gave an answer devised to confront him with his sin and his need of forgiveness. It was imperative that he perceive his sinfulness. People cannot come to Jesus Christ for salvation merely on the basis of psychological needs, anxieties, lack of peace, a sense of hopelessness, an absence of joy, or a yearning for happiness. Salvation is for people who hate their sin and want to turn away from it. It is for individuals who understand that they have lived in rebellion against a holy God and who want to live for His glory.

Jesus' answer took the focus off the young man's felt need and put it back on God: "There is only One who is good." Then He held him against the divine standard so he would see how far short he fell: "If you wish to enter into life, keep the commandments." But the young man ignored and rejected the point. He was utterly unwilling to confess his own sinfulness.

Evangelism must take the sinner and measure him against the perfect law of God so he can see his deficiency. A gospel that deals only with human needs, feelings, and problems is superficial and powerless to save since it focuses only on the symptoms rather than sin, the real issue. That's why churches are filled with people whose lives are essentially no different after professing faith in Christ. Many of those people, I'm sad to say, are unregenerate and grievously misled.

A Call for Repentance

The rich young ruler asked Jesus which commandments he should keep. The Lord responded by giving him the easy half of the Ten Commandments: "You shall not commit murder; You shall not commit adultery; You shall not steal; You shall not bear false witness; Honor your father and mother." Then He adds, "You shall love your neighbor as yourself" (vv. 18 19).

Scripture says, "The young man said to Him, 'All these things I have kept; what am I still lacking?'" (v. 20). That demonstrates his shallow perception of the law. It's possible that on the surface he did all those things, but God looks for an internal application. There was no way he could honestly say he had always kept that law. He could not have been telling the truth-he was either lying or totally self-deluded.

And so, there was no way the rich young ruler could be saved. Salvation is not for people who simply want to avoid hell and gain heaven instead; it is sinners who recognize how unfit they are for heaven and come to God for forgiveness. If you are not ashamed of your sin, you cannot receive salvation.

At this point, Mark 10:21 says, "And looking at him, Jesus felt a love for him." That statement paints a pathetic picture. The young man was sincere. His spiritual quest was genuine. He was an honestly religious person. And Jesus loved him. However, the Lord Jesus does not take sinners on their own terms. As much as He loved the young man, He nevertheless did not grant him eternal life merely because he requested it.

Submission to Christ

Jesus lovingly tried to help the young man see another essential element of salvation: "Jesus said to Him, 'If you wish to be complete, go and sell your possessions and give to the poor, and you shall have treasure in heaven; and come, follow Me' (v. 21). Challenging him, Jesus was basically saying, "You say you love your neighbor as yourself. OK, give him everything you've got. If you really love him as much as you love yourself, that should be no problem."

Jesus was simply testing whether he was willing to submit himself to Christ. Scripture never records that He demanded anyone else sell everything and give it away. The Lord was exposing the man's true weakness-the sin of covetousness, indulgence, and materialism. He was indifferent to the poor. He loved his possessions. So, the Lord challenged that.

Verse 22 says, "When the young man heard this statement, he went away grieved; for he was one who owned much property." He wouldn't come to Jesus if it meant giving up his possessions. It's interesting that he went away grieved. He really did want eternal life; he just wasn't willing to pay the price of repenting of sin and submitting to Christ.

The story has a tragic, heartbreaking ending. The rich young ruler came for eternal life, but left without it. He thought he was rich, but walked away from Jesus with nothing. Although salvation is a blessed gift from God, Christ will not give it to a man whose hands are filled with other things. A person who is not willing to turn from his sin, his possessions, his false religion, or his selfishness will find he cannot turn in faith to Christ.

Adapted from The Gospel According to Jesus by John MacArthur. © Copyright 1988 by John F. MacArthur, Jr.

Used by permission.

Are the Ten Commandments for Today?

I read this from the Voice in the Wilderness on what other Preachers said in reference to it.

I was convicted!

God's definition of sin has never changed. 1 John 3:4 says,
"Sin is the transgression of the law."

When it comes to presenting the Gospel, the greatest minds in the history of the church understood the vital relationship between law and grace.

The Apostle Paul: "Therefore by the deeds of the law no flesh will be justified in His sight, for by the law is the knowledge of sin (Rom. 3:20)." Paul also stated in, (Rom. 7:7)

"What shall we say then? Is the law sin? Certainly not! On the contrary, I would not have known sin except through the law. For I would not have known covetousness unless the law had said, "You shall not covet!"

Charles Spurgeon, who was called the Prince of Preachers in England, back in the 1800's. "I do not believe that any man can preach the gospel who does not preach the Law. The Law is the needle, and you cannot draw the silken thread of the gospel through a man's heart unless you first send the needle of the Law to make way for it. If men do not understand the Law, they will not feel they are sinners. And if they are not consciously sinners, they will never value the sin offering. There is no healing a man till the Law has wounded him, no making him alive till the Law has slain him".

John MacArthur: "Evangelism must take the sinner and measure him against the perfect law of God so he can see his deficiency. A gospel that deals only with human need, only with human feelings, only with human problems, lacks the true balance. That is why churches are full of people whose lives are essentially unchanged after their supposed conversion".

"Most of these people, I am convinced, are unregenerate and grievously misled. We need to adjust our presentation of the gospel. We cannot dismiss the fact that God hates sin and punishes sinners with eternal torment. How can we begin a gospel presentation by telling people on their way to Hell that God has a wonderful plan for their lives? Scripture says, "God is angry with the wicked every day" (Ps. 7:11, KJV).

John Wesley: When speaking of those who didn't use the Law as a school-master, Wesley said, "All these proceeds from the deepest ignorance of the nature of the properties and use of the Law. And, proves that those who act thus either know not Christ, are strangers to living faith, or are at least but babes in Christ, and as such are unskilled in the word of righteousness."

Martin Luther: "The first duty of the gospel preacher is to declare God's Law and show the nature of sin. Why? Because it will act as a schoolmaster and bring him to everlasting life which is in Jesus Christ". Here's another one. "The Law and the gospel are given to the end that we may learn to know both how guilty we are, and to what again we should return."

D.L. Moody: "This is what God gives us the Law for, to show us ourselves and our true colors".

Matthew Henry: "There is no way of coming to that knowledge of sin which is necessary to repentance, but by comparing our hearts and lives by the Law". He also said, "Only a fool would think any method of conviction better than the one God has chosen and appointed."

John Bunyan: "The man who does not know the nature of the Law cannot know the nature of sin. And he who does not know the nature of sin cannot know the nature of the Savior".

Augustine: "Through the Law, God opens man's eyes so that he sees his helplessness and by faith takes refuge to His mercy and is healed. The Law was given in order that we might seek grace, grace was given in order that we might fulfill the Law".

Jonathan Edwards: "What good is it to have godly principles yet not know them? Why should God reveal His mind to us if we don't care enough to know what it is? Yet the only way we can know whether we are sinning is by knowing His moral law: By the law is the knowledge of sin (Rom. 3:20)".

General William Booth: "The chief danger of the Twentieth Century will be religion without the Holy Ghost, Christianity without Christ, forgiveness without repentance, salvation without regeneration, politics without God... and heaven without hell".

J.C. Ryle: "The plain truth is that a right knowledge of sin lies at the root of all saving Christianity. Without it, such doctrines as justification, conversion, sanctification, are `words and names' which convey no meaning to the mind. "The first thing, therefore, that God does when He makes anyone a new creature in Christ, is to send light into his heart and show him that he is a guilty sinner. The material creation in Genesis began with `light,' and so also does the spiritual creation. "God shines into our hearts by the work of the Holy Spirit, and then spiritual life begins.

Leon Morris: "The law of Moses is not a religion of salvation; it is the categorical imperative of God by which men are accused and exposed as sinners".

D. James Kennedy: "You cannot commit a sin outside of the Ten Commandments."

Kay Arthur: "The Old Covenant is the Law which came by Moses, and, believe it or not, it plays a vital role in bringing a man or woman to Christ. If we would use it more, we would probably not have so many false professions of salvation". Got this from: http://bit.ly/2kZFC6Q

Now let us not forget!

Adolph Hitler: "The curse of Mt. Sinai, (Where Moses Received the Ten Commandments) must be gotten out of our blood. It is a poison which has spoiled the free instincts of man."

Hear Ye, Hear Ye, All Rise, Court in Session

Opening statement for the Defense:

Your Honor, ladies and gentlemen of the jury, I will now present my case by examining eyewitnesses from the New Testament.

These witnesses will provide irrefutable proof that Jesus used a method of evangelism that has been, for all practical purposes, entirely forsaken by modern evangelical methods.

In addition, we will provide you (the jury) with expert testimonies from a number of the world's foremost leading authorities in the art and science of Biblical interpretation. This will substantiate our claim, that there is one method of presenting the Gospel that is ordained by God, and as such, cannot be improved upon by man. My final witness will be none other than the Lord Jesus Christ Himself!

FOR MY FIRST WITNESS, I CALL THE RICH YOUNG RULER TO THE STAND . . .

Defense: Will you please tell the court your full name and the story of your encounter with Jesus?

Rich Ruler: My name is Richard Young. When I saw Jesus, I ran up to Him and fell on my knees before Him. I said, "Good teacher, what must I do to inherit eternal life?"

"Why do you call Me good? Jesus answered, "No one is good—except God alone. You know the commandments: `Do not murder, do not commit adultery, do not steal, do not give false testimony, do not defraud, honor your father and mother." "Teacher," I declared, "all these I have kept since I was a youth." Jesus looked at me and loved me. "One thing you lack," He said, "Go, sell everything you have and give to the poor, and you will have treasure in heaven. Then come, follow Me." At this my face fell. I went away sad, because I had great wealth (Mark 10:17–22).

Defense: Your honor, ladies and gentleman of the jury, this was written for our instruction. A man comes to Jesus Christ and asks, "What must I do to be saved?"

The first thing Jesus did was to list 5 of the Ten Commandments. Obviously, the moral law must have something to do with evangelism! Take another look. The man asks, "What must I do to be saved?"

Jesus replied, "You know the law. Thou shalt not murder, thou shalt not commit adultery, thou shalt not steal, thou shalt not lie, honor your father and your mother."

Jesus purposely omitted the tenth commandment which is, "Thou shalt not covet." The rich young ruler then says, "All these things I have done since I was a youth, what am I still lacking?"

Now comes the final blow. Jesus said, "Go sell everything you have and give it to the poor." Rather than quoting the tenth commandment (which is "thou shalt not covet"), Jesus applied the text directly to his heart by asking a covetous person to do something a covetous person would not do! In order to reveal the true condition of his heart, Jesus Christ used the Ten Commandments as His standard!

Defense: WARREN WIERSBE, TO THE STAND

Mr. Wiersbe, you are recognized the world over as an expert Bible commentator. How do you interpret this story?

Warren Wiersbe: "The rich ruler is a good example of the use of the law to reveal sin and show a man his need of a Savior.

1. Why did Jesus bring up the commandments? Jesus did not introduce the law to show the young man how to be saved, but to show him that *he needed to be saved*.

2. When Jesus quoted from the second table of the law, He did not quote the last commandment, 'Thou shalt not covet'

(Ex. 20:17). Jesus knew the young man's heart

3. This young man was possessed by the love of money and he would not let go. He wanted salvation on his terms, not God's, so he turned and went away in great sorrow."

Defense: No further questions.

Judge: Would the State like to cross-examine?

State: Ah, not at this time, your Honor.

Judge: You may step down. Next witness.

Defense: Your Honor, in 1910, A.C. Gaebelein produced a commentary that is still considered one of the most authoritative works ever produced on the book of Matthew. Mr. Gaebelein, do you have anything to add to what Mr. Wiersbe has testified to?

A.C. Gaebelein: I certainly do. Thank you. Your Honor, ladies and gentlemen of the jury.

4. "The Lord meets him on his own ground. The ground upon which he stands is the law, and with the law the Lord answers his question. How else could He treat him? The first need for him was to know himself a lost and helpless sinner. If the Lord had spoken of His grace, of eternal life as a free gift, he would not have understood Him at all. The law was needed to make known to him his desperate condition and to lay bare his heart."

Defense: Thank you, Mr. Gaebelein. Your Honor, Jesus said to the rich young ruler, "Go, sell everything you have and give it to the poor." How would that have helped him? Would he have been saved if he had gone out and given everything he had to the poor? Never! In spirit and in truth, this "command" to go and sell all he had and give it to the poor was given to reveal to him (and to us) the fact that his goods were his gods!

The Rich Young Ruler was in clear violation of the first (no other gods), the second (no idols), and the tenth (not to covet) commandments. The very law he thought he kept only revealed the true condition of his heart. "For where your treasure is, there your heart will be also" (Matt.6:21).

State: I object, on the grounds of hyper-dispensationalism. Nothing in the Bible is relevant to the Christian today prior to the Book of Acts!

Defense: Ah, your Honor, Paul said in

Galatians 3:24 that, "The law is our schoolmaster to lead us to Christ that we might be justified (saved) by faith" (KJV). That was *after* the Book of Acts! This hyper-dispensationalist doctrine is heresy!

Judge: Overruled!!! Proceed.

Defense: For my next witness, I call the woman at the well. Madam, would you please tell the court your experience with Jesus on that fateful day?

Samaritan Woman: Well, as you know, I'm a Samaritan and a woman. I came to draw water from the well one day, and Jesus said to me, "Will you give me a drink?" (His disciples had gone into the town to buy food.) I said to Him, "You are a Jew and I am a Samaritan woman. How can You ask me for a drink?" (For Jews do not associate with Samaritans.)

He replied: "If you knew the gift of God and who it is that asks you for a drink, you would have asked Me and I would have given you living water (John 4:10).

"Sir," I said, "You have nothing to draw with and the well is deep. Where can you get this living water? Are you greater than our father Jacob, who gave us the well and drank from it himself, as did also his sons and his flocks and herds" (vss. 11,12)?

Jesus answered: "Everyone who drinks this water will be thirsty again, but whoever drinks the water I give him will never thirst. Indeed, the water I give him will become in him a spring of water welling up to eternal life (vss. 13,14).

At this point, I got excited. I said to Him, "Sir, give me this water so that I won't get thirsty and have to keep coming here to draw water" (vs. 15). Jesus said to me, "Go, call your husband and come back" (vs. 16). "I have no husband," I replied.

He then said, "You are right when you say you have no husband. The fact is, you have had five husbands, and the man you now have is not your husband (vss. 17,18).

"What you have just said is quite true, Sir," I replied. "I can see that You are a prophet" (vs. 19). Then, leaving my water jar, I went back to the town and said to the people, "Come, see a man who told me everything I ever did. Could this be the Christ" (vss. 28,29)?

Defense: Your Honor, this woman asked Jesus for the living water, so she would never have to thirst again. The problem here is that she was talking about H2O, and He was talking about the Holy Spirit. Please note, the woman asked Jesus for a drink, and He did *not* give it to her!

The lesson is clear. The average "would-be" soul winner, upon hearing her request for a drink (completely oblivious to the fact that they were talking about two different things), would have immediately pulled out a tract and started offering her all the benefits of the Gospel before she understood why she needed it!

Jesus did not give her the "water," because she did not understand that ultimately her real need was not water, but the "washing with the water through the word" (Eph. 5:26). Specifically, her real need was the conviction, confession, repentance, and forgiveness of sin!

Because the sin problem had not been dealt with yet, Jesus went right to the heart of the problem. When she said, "Give me a drink," He said, "Go call your husband!" On the surface, His answer seems irrelevant. What did calling her husband have to do with getting a drink? Everything! Look again. Jesus said, "Go call your husband." She said, "I have no husband."

Jesus replied, "You are correct, Madam. You have had five husbands, and the man you are *living with now is not* your husband!"

She brilliantly responded with, "Sir, I perceive that Thou art a prophet!" What was Jesus doing? Make no mistake about it. Just like the rich young ruler, Jesus was asking this woman to do something a fornicator and an adulterer could not do.

The Lord was referring her (and us) to the seventh commandment, which is "Thou shalt not commit adultery." Why? Because from Genesis to Revelation, God's Word assures us that those who do not repent from the practice of sexual immorality will not enter the kingdom of heaven!

Or do you not know that the unrighteous shall not inherit the kingdom of God? Do not be deceived; neither *fornicators*, nor idolaters, nor adulterers, nor effeminate, nor homosexuals, nor thieves, nor {the} covetous, nor drunkards, nor revilers, nor swindlers, shall inherit the kingdom of God (1 Cor. 6: 9–10).

Judge: Would the State like to cross-examine?

State: Ah, no, your Honor. This doesn't exactly fit my theology, but I don't know how to refute it.

Judge: Very well. Call your next witness, Counselor.

5. Defense: I call Nicodemus to the stand. Nic, you were there. Tell us your story.

Nicodemus: Well, I'm a Pharisee and my full name is Nicodemus. I'm a member of the Jewish ruling council. I came to Jesus at night and said, "Rabbi, we know you are a teacher who has come from God. For no one could perform the miraculous signs you are doing if God were not with him." In reply, Jesus declared,

Truly, truly, I say to you, unless one is born again, he cannot see the kingdom of God (vs. 3).

Then I asked Him, "How can a man be born when he is old? He cannot enter a second time into his mother's womb and be born, can he?"

Jesus said: I tell you the truth, no one can enter the kingdom of God unless he is born of water and the Spirit. Flesh gives birth to flesh, but the Spirit gives birth to spirit. (John 3:1–6).

Defense: Thank you, Nicodemus. You may step down. I would now like to call one of the greatest Bible commentators of the 20th century to the stand. I call Arthur W. Pink. Arthur, what can you tell us about this most curious exchange between Jesus and Nicodemus?

6. A.W. Pink: Well, here is what I wrote in my commentary on John, word for word:

"What the sinner needs is to be 'born again,' and in order to do this he must have a Savior. And it is of these very things our Lord speaks to Nicodemus. Of what value is teaching to one who is 'dead in trespasses and sins,' and who is even now, under the condemnation of a holy God!

"A saved person is a fit subject for teaching, but what the unsaved need is preaching, preaching which will expose their depravity, exhibit their deep need of a Savior, and then and only then reveal the one who is mighty to save."

Defense: Thank you, Mr. Pink. Judge, here again we see the same pattern. Jesus asked Nicodemus to do something he could not do.

So, where do we see the law in this instance? The key word here, is the word *Pharisee*. The typical Pharisee thought his salvation was based on the fact that he was a descendent of Abraham. He believed he was on a one-way trip to heaven, based solely on his national and religious heritage (by keeping the *law* of Moses). His theology was totally backwards.

Nicodemus thought he was an in-law, when in fact he was an outlaw. The Bible assures us that God does not have any grandchildren. According to [Romans 3:20](), the law that this Pharisee thought would save him was the very law that would condemn him!

With that one statement, "You must be born again," Jesus was referring Nicodemus to his misunderstanding of the Law. No one was *ever* saved by keeping it, because the perfect law demanded perfect obedience. "The law," as Leon Morris has pointed out, "is the categorical imperative of God, by which men are accused and exposed as sinners."

Human nature has not changed since the beginning of time, and will remain the same until the end. The people to whom Jesus witnessed were caught up in the same self-righteousness, self-justification, and love of the world as we are today. The names have changed, but the sin nature has not. So, what do we learn from these examples?

THESE THREE PEOPLE REPRESENT THE VAST MAJORITY OF THE PEOPLE YOU WILL ENCOUNTER IN WITNESSING

1. Nicodemus believed his salvation was in religion.

2. The woman at the well was blinded by her sin, and unaware of her true spiritual condition.

3. The rich young ruler thought he was a good person.

Jesus referred each of them directly or indirectly to the Ten Commandments!

THERE IS ONE EXCEPTION TO USING THE LAW

7. If you meet a person under condemnation, who really believes his past is so bad that God Himself cannot or will not forgive him, *this person does not need the law.* There is only one thing standing between this person and everlasting life, a crystal-clear understanding of grace!

Remember the woman caught in the very act of adultery in John. 8:4? Jesus asked her, "Where are those who condemn you?" She said, "There are none Lord." Jesus replied,

"Neither do I condemn you. Go and sin no more."

Bengel: Those who are broken and contrite Jesus consoles with the Gospel, but to the proud and self-righteous He gave the law. Your Honor, before offering my closing arguments, I would like to ask Jesus to reveal the truth one more time. Lord?

Jesus: "Now there was a certain rich man, and he habitually dressed in purple and fine linen, gaily living in splendor every day. And a certain poor man named Lazarus was laid at his gate, covered with sores, and longing to be fed with the {crumbs} which were falling from the rich man's table; besides, even the dogs were coming and licking his sores.

Now it came about that the poor man died and he was carried away by the angels to Abraham's bosom; and the rich man also died and was buried. And in Hades he lifted up his eyes, being in torment, and saw Abraham far away, and Lazarus in his bosom. And he cried out and said, `Father Abraham, have mercy on me, and send Lazarus, that he may dip the tip of his finger in water and cool off my tongue; for I am in agony in this flame.'

But Abraham said, `Child, remember that during your life you received your good things, and likewise Lazarus bad things; but now he is being comforted here, and you are in agony.' And besides all this, between us and you there is a great chasm fixed, in order that those who wish to come over from here to you may not be able, and {that} none may cross over from there to us.'

And he said, `Then I beg you, Father, that you send him to my father's house—for I have five brothers—that he may warn them, lest they also come to this place of torment.' But Abraham said, `They have Moses and the Prophets; let them hear them.' But he said, `No, Father Abraham, but if someone goes to them from the dead, they will repent!' But he said to him, `If they do not listen to Moses and the Prophets, neither will they be persuaded if someone rises from the dead'"

(Luke 16:19-31).

At this point, pandemonium broke out! Reporters ran to the phones to get the story out as quickly as possible.

Jesus Himself had just said that using the law of Moses in the evangelistic encounter was a more compelling argument for Christianity than someone rising from the dead!

The lawyer for the A.C.L.U. just hung his head and the judge was banging his gavel, calling for order in the court! When order was finally restored, the judge asked me to proceed, and I closed with this.

Defense: Your Honor, ladies and gentleman of the jury, (Luke 16) is crystal-clear. Jesus, in relating this story, is saying in no uncertain terms that you have a better chance of leading people to Christ by introducing them first to Moses than if their own grandmother came back from the dead to warn them of the judgment to come!

By God's grace, Matthew Henry, one of the most respected commentators of all time, understood this last verse perfectly. He said, "Foolish men are apt to think any method of conviction better than that which God has chosen and appointed." The inevitable result of the knowledge of sin, is an overwhelming sense of gratitude for God's past, present, and future grace. This in turn produces a passion for loving obedience and a hatred for sin.

At this point, we want to obey God not to get saved, but because salvation has already been provided; not in a law, but in a Person, and that Person is Jesus Christ!

FOR YOUR INFORMATION

You can be certain that the Ten Commandments were written by God and not by man, because if man wrote them, there would be ten commandments and a thousand amendments. You can be sure they are divine, because every man from the beginning of time until the end of the world, whether or not he has ever read a Bible or ever heard of Jesus Christ, knows in his heart it's wrong to murder, it's wrong to steal, it's wrong to lie, and it's wrong to have another man's wife!

How else can you explain the fact that this moral standard is universally accepted as true and right? Only a fool would not agree. You can believe that the Ten Commandments are divinely inspired, because between them and every other religion, philosophy, or system of thought, there is no possible term of comparison.

Think about it. (Galatians 5:14) (which is a distillation of the Ten Commandments), says: "For all the Law is fulfilled in one word, even in this: `You shall love your neighbor as yourself.'" If we all cared about each other as much as we cared about ourselves, we would live in a perfect world! I rest my case.

Judge: Does the State have anything at all?

State: Yes, I want to get saved!

Judge: This court is forced to the inescapable conclusion, based on Scripture and reason, that the New Testament is crystal clear on the place of the Ten Commandments in evangelism.

Beginning with Moses and explaining the New Testament application of each one of the Ten Commandments in the evangelistic encounter, is the most compelling and convicting method of preparing the heart for the message of God's love and mercy. Furthermore, since this is the method that Christ Himself used, and since nobody knows more about evangelism than Jesus, I hereby declare, by the authority of the Word of God, that, in the words of one evangelist,

Evermore, the law must prepare the way for the Gospel. To overlook this in instructing souls is almost certain to result in false hope, the introduction of a false standard of Christian experience and to fill the church with false converts.

In closing, it is clear that God did not leave us to fend for ourselves in presenting His most precious truth. But rather, over the course of some 1,500 years, from Sinai to the cross, gave us a perfect picture of His own systematic theology of evangelism. As such, it cannot be improved upon by any man or man-made institution, no matter who they may be. "Thanks be to God, for His indescribable gift" (2 Cor. 9:15).

My judgment is for the defense. Next case!

Tennis Anyone 2005

Tennis, why mention tennis?

Well after a several years attending a mega Church, with about five thousand members, I saw how they would try to get church members, their friends and families to play games, such as golf, or basketball, so they can share with them what their Church is about. Being a well-rounded tennis player and teacher, I thought why not host a tennis tournament of my own through the Church venue.

I was amazed that my church approved me to do it! Even a private club allowed me, without even being a member. This included being able to reserve several courts on a day a month ahead to have the event. This only was truly a blessing from the Lord as no one would be able to reserve courts without membership and a month in advance. These courts are for the paying members only.

The three Sundays prior to the event I would stand outside the Church entrance with a sign-up sheet and was able to get the players needed to fill the courts. They had to pay $10.00 and would get a free lunch, as well as prizes. Family and friends were also invited to watch and receive a free lunch.

Another amazing Hand of the Lord at work was that many times I would be short the necessary four players on a court. Low and behold some would show up not having signed up, and the court would be complete with four players. I hope you can see that my desire was to reach out to as many people as I could by using this game of tennis as the conduit to those who attended. I did this about three times a year for about three years. While they were having lunch, I would present a Gospel message that hinged on my testimony and how it has affected my life.

This was based on what I came to believe to be true about what my conversion meant. Now I was one who had repented of my sins, placed my trust in Jesus Christ alone for the forgiveness of them. Now being Born Again, adopted into the Kingdom and eternally saved from the depths of Hell was compelled to share with others.

Sadly, near the end I was told not to share my testimony with this group as that is not what the Church does. Imagine getting a phone call from the head of the Men's Ministry telling you NOT to give your testimony or share the Gospel at the event. I was told that no one did that at any of the other sporting events that the Church sponsored and those events were only for fellowship. I told him if I could not give my testimony, I would not host the events.

Amazing he stated that I should keep doing it. Everyone he talks to mentioned that they really liked it. That's when I said why are you trying to stop me from putting in on and sharing. He finally stated that one of the men that is his friend, didn't like me sharing at the event. He thought it should only be done with the intention of having fellowship. Everyone who attends comes from Church and probably already are Christians, and they don't need to hear it again.

Amazing how one man's flawed opinion is held in such high esteem that even an Elder of a Mega Church accepts it because of friendship.

Praise the Lord as what came to me was to ask him to come to next event and if I'm saying anything that's unbiblical then he can stop me. Well it happened, he came for a little while and never said anything to me about stopping. It.

Boot Camp in Seattle Washington

Drawing a crowd by offering money to anyone who can prove they are a Good Person

Chris in Las Vegas, June 2006

*T*his is when I meet Ray and Kirk for the first time.

This was a weekend of getting together for prayer with others who were willing to get out of their comfort zone and go out amongst the crowds in the streets and publicly proclaim the Gospel.

Ray showed us a simple way to draw a crowd was by asking trivia question and giving away money if they guess the right answer.

Amazing how many will stop to try to win the money. When that person does, then the next question we asked is, "Would they consider themselves to be a good person?"

One of the amazing encounters was on the street in Vegas where a young man named, "Chris" wanted to take the Good Person Test. Proclaiming his goodness, I asked him if it would be okay if I used God's Ten Commandments to validate his claim so that I would not be judging him. He agreed and failed miserably, and then when I asked innocent or guilty in God's eyes, here it comes, "INNOCENT!" When I ask how can that be if he violated 4 of the Commandments. He then stated he was a Christian and God is a loving and forgiving God.

Next I explained that God was also a Righteous and Just God and must punish liars, thief's, blasphemies or He's Not God. Well for the rest of the story please go to my webpage, **www.tillthenetsRFull.org** where you can watch what happened.

This again to me was another blessing as I have been told by those that I attended church with, that people would not want a video of them while taking this test…you can now observe that they are wrong!

A Suggestion on how NOT to get OFFENDED

During my worldly years before becoming adopted in the Kingdom of God, this phase was foremost in my mind.

"Advise not asked for is advise not worth giving"

But in 1994 that all changed. The scripture is clear, that we are to be one with one another and to share with others. So, I have decided to share with you what the Lord has given me to help with my relationship with others. This is not my brainstorm as I'm not that smart. I got it from a reliable source, a wise man who also is a Brother in Christ.

Several years ago, I was blessed to be able to speak with a Dallas Demmitt, PH.D. He wrote a book called:

"Can You Hear Me Now?" written with his wife Nancy.

On the front cover, Gary Smalley states,
"Prepare to experience the power of listening."

After reading what Dallas Demmitt wrote in his book, "Can You Hear Me Now?", what came to me was these (7) - (4) - (3) words. You will read what they are in a little while. They should be, ***internalized***! This could change any and all of your relationships with those who are close to you, as well as anyone else you meet.

For those of us who believe God's Word:
Proverbs 12:1 states,

"Whoever loves discipline loves knowledge, but he who hates reproof is stupid."

Now please remember, I'm not calling anyone stupid, so, let's not get OFFENDED!

Paul states, " Do nothing from rivalry or conceit, but in humility count others more significant than yourselves. Let each of you look not only to his own interests, but also to the interests of others. Have this mind among yourselves, which is yours in Christ Jesus, who, though he was in the form of God, did not count equality with God a thing to be grasped, but made himself nothing, taking the form of a servant, being born in the likeness of men. And being found in human form, he humbled himself by becoming obedient to the point of death, even death on a cross. (Philippians 2:3-8)

So, here's the scenario:

Let's say that someone states that you are, " you fill in the blanks", as a negative observation or of something that pertains to you. Again, I need your help on this. Is it not true that the typical response from anyone who makes a negative statement about you, that you would naturally defend yourself?

When someone says something about you, whether a praise or a criticism, your response should be these (7) words. By repeating these (7) words you are validating and clarifying what that person said about you instead of what typically happens is, that you defend yourself.

"Is that what you see in me?"

But He gives a greater grace. Therefore, it says,
"GOD IS OPPOSED TO THE PROUD,
BUT GIVES GRACE TO THE HUMBLE." (James 4:6)

So how could we apply the above information? It's stated in (James 5:19-20)? Shouldn't we be more concerned about speaking the truth? Speaking the truth would be honoring God, and we should be more concerned about honoring God than honoring others. If we are truly concerned about others destiny, offending them or us being offended, should not be our concern. I've sadly heard, that being truthful is equivalent to, being judgmental!

My brethren, if any among you strays from the truth and one turns him back, let him know that he who turns a sinner from the error of his way will save his soul from death and will cover a multitude of sins. (James 5:19-20)

So back to those (7) words again. If we respond with them can't you see the freedom you allow your loved ones and friends to have when they need to express what they have in their heart about you? Once you get those (7) words internalized, NOT memorized, as you must be able to respond with them, then you're ready for the next (4) words.

"Is there anything else?"

Now that's really brave, but I hope you can see the humility that comes from such a response. You are allowing another person to tell you what they observe in your behavior, attitude or demeanor. Wouldn't that be helpful to see ourselves as others see us?

Now you're ready to graduate, for its now time for the (3) words, that really place you in a humble place.

" Is there more?"

Once you have reached this plateau then you can humbly ask that person to pray for you because you shouldn't want to be like that. Again, I can only pray that you would a least get the book and try to apply his concept on how to improve your listen skills and possible you may never be OFFENDED again.

Japan Mission Trip – January 2008

Catherine and I have been blessed by God to be able to go to Japan to Spread the Gospel.

I did not know that Japan is dominated by two major religions, Shinto and Buddhism. Christians in Japan are in a distinct minority, so mission trips to this country do much to nurture and grow and spread the beautiful Gospel message of Jesus The Christ. We are just two nobodies who can share with everybody about somebody that can save anybody.

Here we are at the Phoenix Arizona airport on Thursday, leaving at 7:30AM and arriving in Tokyo Japan on Friday at 5:30PM. There we will meet David Spurdle. He is the one who invited us to go and has his Missionary in Japan. Then we took three separate trains to get to where he parked his van. This took approximately another two hours. Then 45 minutes later we arrived at the house where we would stay, this was about 8:30 or 9PM Japan time. That meant that we had been up for about 27 hours, (as it was now 5:am, Friday Phoenix time.)

On the first train our prayers were answered as we had been praying that the Lord would bring people to us who spoke English.

Catherine handing out her first Million Dollar Gospel Tract to this man on the train going to Tochigi

At the first stop this man got on and sat next to Catherine. He asked her if she would mind if he sat by her. She was surprised how well he spoke English and complimented him on it. She then offered him a million and he took it. After reading it, he mentioned that he liked the Tract and that he was a Christian and she continued to have a great conversation with him. He gave us the newspaper he had with him as it was written in English and he stated that he buys it so that he would better understand the English language. Praise the Lord for answering our prayers.

Here we are with our team in Tochigi

Saturday. January, 26 (which is Friday in Phoenix) Woke up early Sat, David made great blueberry pancakes. Each day after breakfast we have a Bible study, and learn about missionaries in Japan. After our study David took us for a walk that lead us to the base of a mountain. We climbed that mountain and at the top we could see the city that Satan held captive. We prayed to the Lord above that He would use us to help free those people and bring truth to the city of Tochigi.

On our way down David and Jack were able to witness to two people, a mother and son who were cleaning the area. Afterwards we went to the mall to buy some supplies and to pass out tracks. They had a Starbucks inside the mall and we were privileged to talk to a young girl named Kazayo, as she spoke English and was able to understand what I was saying.

Knowing she would understand me, I walked her through four of the Ten Commandments. She was convicted by the law and Catherine noticed that she had tears in her eyes when we got to the part where she stated that would it concerned her that she could be in Hell.

David invited her to his home for that night as his pastor and the pastor's son were coming that night. To my amazement she and her sister showed up. Afterwards we all went to dinner at a great Japanese restaurant and shared with one another. Jack and I started singing and were having a grand time coming up with all the different songs that we could remember. Even the owners who were the cook and his wife were smiling at us singing.

Sunday, 27th, Here we are attending worship at the chapel in Tochigi and we all shared our testimonies. Afterwards I was able to log on to my website and share the video of a man using rubber balls to play music on the piano that was on the floor.

I also shared with them the Red and Blue illusion cards. When you hold them apart like in the picture below you will see that the one on the top left is the Red one and it looks bigger than the Blue one below it. But when I place the Blue one above the Red one then the Blue one looks bigger. I also show them with one on the top of the other and they appear the same size. If you look at the lower image you will see that the longer curved side facing each other is why they look the same size. That's why when you place the shorter curved side next to the longer curved side, they look different.

That's when they start to stare and wonder how can that be? The next step in showing this illusion is so you can ask them this question. Being that you see them as being different and yet I can also show you they are the same, "I guess your eyes can fool you, can't they?" Of course, they respond with, "YES!" Sometimes we can just hand them the cards and tell them if they would like to know why their eyes can fool them just read the back. Be sure to read the card that has Card One on it first, as it will explain why it's happening. This has the opportunity to have them read about what God expects from us to be Born Again.

Other times we can read what it says on the back to them as it winds up asking them if they are good enough to get into Heaven? We only need four of God's Ten Commandments to validate if they qualify to get into Heaven or Hell.

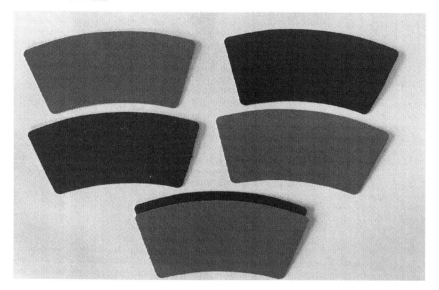

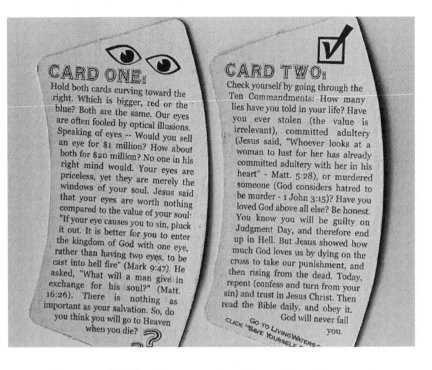

If you would like to have some : http://store.livingwaters.com/

We were invited to a ladies' home which was on the outskirts which was like a farm house. She served us an amazing meal which Catherine helped her to prepare. She shared with Catherine all about her two sons and then took Catherine to her bedroom where she showed her pictures of her daughter in beautiful Japanese gowns.

Monday, 28th We drove to the top of another mountain, Ohira, in Tochigi. We had a terrific view of Tokyo in the distance and could even see Mt Fuji. They have a three-story platform that you can walk up to get a better view and there we saw padlocks that were engraved and locked into the fence that surrounded the platform. I was told by Jack that couples who want to get married leave them there. As we looked out over the area David had us pray for all of those people who have never heard of the Gospel. We drove around the area where the church is and dropped off flyers inviting people to come to the church on Saturday.

Tuesday, 29th Today was a damp and rainy day. Even children get excited about the many Gospel Tracts. We dropped off Tracts locally and then went to the mall and stopped at Starbucks.

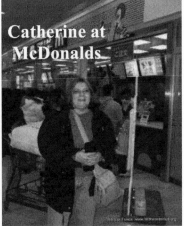

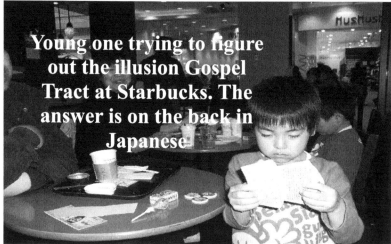

These two young ladies were visibly effected when taking the Good Person Test.

Look how excited this family is about receiving a Million Dollar Gospel Tract!

While walking around David was able to share with a man who stated that he had never heard the Gospel before. With the Lords help, and our Million Dollar Gospel tract, David was able to help this man complete the connection from the old Chinese manuscripts on how God and His begotten Son Jesus was real.

Wednesday 30th Today we drove to Mt Nikko, where there is a Christian camp. We actually have a bed to sleep on and heat on the floors. We all went to a tiny hut where we prayed for Haruko who is the wife of the Pastor at Tochigi as she has a failing liver.

Praying for the Pastors wife, "Haruko" who has a failing liver

We also prayed over Nakajima, a close friend of theirs who has ovarian cancer and was told she only had a year to live. Then we split up and each went to their own little hut for about an hour to spend some quiet time with the Lord.

We then drove to a place called Nikko Wonderland, but the attraction was closed from Jan.25-Feb.7, we just missed it. While we wondering around at this empty location some college students from Tokyo showed up. We were able to witness to them for quite a while. When they left to get on their bus, they we very thankful that we shared, the Million Dollar Gospel Tracts, with JFK on the front and the Japanese language on the back. Needless to say, they were very well received.!

When we came back to the camp, we were able to use the hot water bath. First everyone goes inside to shower and then steps into a large bath and from there you go outside to another large hot bath which is located on the edge of the small canyon. From this spot you could see a water fall which falls into the river below. AWESOME!

After dinner we had prayer time and Bible study. This was an unplanned part of our trip as we were asked by Haga San the Pastor if we would accompany them so that we could pray to the Lord for the two women for their healing.

Thursday, 31st Then next morning we went to the Nikko Tokugawa Shrine. This place is amazing! The buildings and their artistic sculptures are truly a work of art. The only problem is that they are art works for Satan. I was told that millions of people come from all over the world to worship here. They even have what looks like the Ark of the Convenient as described in the Old Testament in one of the temples.

The five of us were able to hand out 100's of Tracts to tourists. Jack the oldest was able to walk up three hundred and fifty-two stairs of the Temple. This could only be accomplished with the Lords power. The rest of us were lazy as we didn't even try to reach the top.

Friday, Feb 1st, got more flyers from the Chapel Headed towards a housing project and put them and the Million Dollar Gospel Tracts in their mailboxes. We then met up with the kids at the park from the last time and played some games with them. Even Jack tried to hit the ball but to no avail.

About a dozen more school kids on bikes came to the park and we able to pass out Million Dollar Gospel Tracts to all of them. They were very excited to have the money and we explained to them that they had to read the back and have their parents do the same.

Group of kids in the park who received Ten Commandment coins & Million Dollar Gospel Tracts

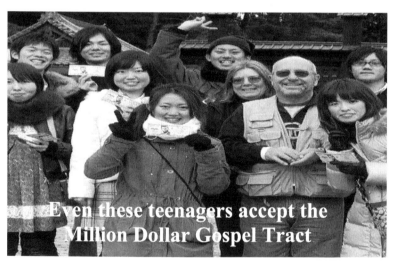

Even these teenagers accept the Million Dollar Gospel Tract

Saturday Feb 2nd, we went to Starbucks again for some more fishing and they had a live band in the mall. As they were performing, I mingled with the crowd and offered them the Million Dollar Gospel Tract. I'm sure they thought it had something to do with the entertainment that was going on because no one refused them. I was able to hand out almost a hundred of them as I emptied the whole pack. Jack came over and helped out as he gave a bunch away as well and then the Mall Security made him stop. By then it was too late as our task of handing out God's word in Satan's domain was complete.

Evening came quickly and we had to get back to our base as we were entertaining some people from his church as well as neighbors that were invited. David and Catherine prepared a wonderful American meal, burritos. They loved it as many had two helpings.

As the evening went on Shin the son of the Pastor Haga asked if I would show his friend the magic. While doing the tricks one of the neighbors asked me to do more and then I showed the Red and Blue illusion and then with the help of David, translating it into Japanese, I took him through the question about selling their eyes. We were able to go through the process of how God would have to judge a sinner, which we know is someone who lies, steals or has lustful thoughts for others. The neighbor's response to it was that, "he never gave it much thought."

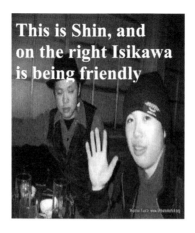

Now comes the amazing part, remember the friend that Shin brought, his name is Isikawa, that's him with his hand up. I noticed that his eyes were wet and he started to speak about how he understood what I was saying and how he is a Buddhist and so is his whole family. He related to us about his grandfather's funeral that when he looked at him lying dead, his face seemed peaceful.

Since then he had been trying to live his life by doing good things just like his grandfather taught him. After hearing what I spoke of he now understood my message and was very thankful for me sharing, as he had never heard anything like this before!

He is still a Buddhist but know wants to search out other religions. I asked if he had every read the Bible and he said no. I then offered him a Bible written in Japanese and he thanked me and said he would read it. His tearful story brought me to ask if I could give him a hug and he responded by leaning over towards me.

I was hugging him he said that he has great respect for me and then I told him that this moment was the best thing that happened to me in Japan and I think that God wanted me here so that he could hear my message. Definitely it was worth the price of coming to Japan. I then told him I would be praying for him so that God would open his heart and he would truly understand why Jesus died on the cross for him. After that I could hardly speak as I realized that God had answered my prayers, and allowed me to hear the heart of someone in Japan.

These are the two who spent time with us. One was the son of a Pastor and the other his Buddhist friend. When he heard why the Law is necessary, he thanked me as it made sense and as being a Buddhist didn't.

Catherine built a snow-woman for the first time ever, the day before we left for home!

On the way home this lady taking the train to Tokyo airport to go to Mexico was excited about receiving the Ten Commandments coin.

Even this stranger, upon arriving in Phoenix AZ, accepts the Million Dollar Gospel Tract!

Niagara Falls

June 2008

Catherine and I are getting ready to leave for Niagara Falls. We will be there until the 15th.

Please pray that God uses us in a mighty way to those we meet both in Canada and the U.S.A. We are taking our weapons to fight a spiritual war by bringing over three thousand Gospel Tracks with the Good Person Test on them. We will be returning on the 23rd of June.

On the plane we chatted with the couple behind us because Catherine thought she heard them speaking about The Way of the Master. They weren't, but we carried on a conversation with them and just before we landed, I showed them the Red and Blue optical illusion card and the couple behind them was also amazed. (Can you see how powerful these Tracts are that even those people who you are not speaking to are in awe and want to know what it's all about.) Needless to say, I gave both couples the Tract and told them to read the back to find out how it worked.

When we landed in Buffalo, I saw two Nuns sitting at the airport and took the opportunity to give them "Which Religion is Right?" Tract. They took them with a smile and then said, "Thank you."

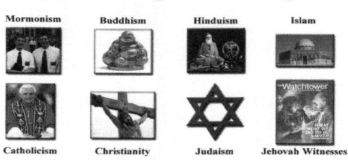

Some say that all religions are just different roads leading to the same place and the same God. But, these religions **totally contradict** each other. They all have very different perceptions of who "God" is. Christianity is the only religion on the front that says eternal life is a free gift. All the others think that you can work for or "earn" your salvation in some way. To understand what I am talking about, let's look at the Ten Commandments: #9 Ever lied? #8 Ever stolen? #3 Ever taken God's name in vain? If you have done these things then you are a liar, a thief and a blasphemer. You are guilty before God and deserve to be punished! That punishment is HELL! No matter how much "good" you have done or will do, you still deserve to be punished for your sins. Your "good" deeds can't wash away your sins! But, God wants to show you **forgiveness, grace and mercy.** That is why He sent His Son, Jesus Christ, to die on the cross for your sins. HE is THE WAY, THE TRUTH and THE LIFE! He is the only way to God! Eternal life is a **FREE GIFT** available to **ALL** who will Repent of their sins and Trust in Jesus Christ. Do it today! For more information go to: www.TillTheNetsRFull.org

HOW AWESOME IS THAT!

It's an honor and a privilege to introduce you to our team members. We had Hans from New York, Joshua from Florida, Ron, Jon, and Tim from Texas (Tim and Jon were our leaders and the ones who arranged this boot camp. dARREL (he spells it this way) and his wife Bernice, and Ken from Washington State, and from Arizona Elaine her daughter Rachel and her husband Mark, as well as their friends Amelia and Mike, who are getting married next week. So, I guess I can say that we had sower's from around the country, half from Arizona!

I thought you might be interested in what our days were like so here is our itinerary.

Every morning breakfast from 7-9 and prayer time till 10.

- **Thursday,** we went to downtown Buffalo from 11-4 and then to Lafayette Square from 7-11p. The crowds were massive; I've never seen that many people in one place! (Now I know what it means when they say "wall to wall people".) Several Open Airs, One-2-Ones and thousands of Tracts were given out as well. (Lots of gang members at Lafayette Square!)
- **Friday,** we went to Niagara Falls (Canada side) from 11-5 and from 8-midnight at the American side. Lots of fish to catch and for god to clean there.
- **Saturday,** went to the Allentown Art Festival in Buffalo from 11-5. We were able to video some of the open airs as well as the one-two-ones. Later I will post them for you to see. later that night we went back to Niagara Falls, Ontario from seven after midnight, and again several open airs and one-two-ones as well.

Each day we had several opportunities with what seemed like hundreds of people who after they took the "Good Person Test", understood the true meaning of why they needed a Savior. Not everyone we spoke to accepted Christ (that's God's part). ***We catch 'em, He cleans 'em!*** That's the freedom of this method of sharing using God's Law, "The Ten Commandments"; it takes the burden of responsibility from us and yet still be an obedient servant of the Lord. (see Mark 16:15)

There were many that when we helped them understand their destiny and that God was not this all forgiving God no matter what they did, we saw their expressions change from prideful arrogance to helplessness. Just about everyone thanked us and were grateful that we took the time to share with them.

Catherine and I would love to thank you for all your prayers! God blessed us immensely by allowing us to come to this Evangelism Boot Camp and proclaim the Gospel of Jesus the Christ.

Click on this link if you want to see more pictures:

They left their homes to come share. **Praying before we go out.** **GREAT FISHING HERE!**

Catherine witnessing to many who may be lost.

A SNAKE, REALLY!

Police asking us to move elsewhere

Family in Canada wanting their picture taking with the Million

This is the Million Dollar Gospel Tract we hand out.

What happened at a Funeral?

December 2008

Since this is to be the season for giving, I thought I would share what happened to me Sunday at a funeral for the Episcopalian priest, (AKA Padre), that's Catherine's family has associated with him and his family for generations.

Last year at this time we went to his wife's funeral. I always carry Million Dollar Gospel Tracts just in case I encounter someone who needs to read one.

I don't really remember how many I passed out but I know I passed out several. I tell you this first so that you might be able to experience how I felt when I was confronted by a woman who is a longtime friend of Catherine's brother. I was listening to her brother speak when this woman came up to me and said, "I know you, you were the one who was handing out those Million Dollar Gospel Tracts, why didn't you give me one?" Needless to say, I was in shock to have someone confront me about what I had done a year ago, and the fact that she remembered me was mind boggling!

I then asked her to forgive me for not giving her one and then handed her one. I then told her to read the back as this is a Gospel Tract and she might want to answer the Million Dollar question, "Are you good enough to get into Heaven?" She thanked me for giving it to her and then said that she was good enough. To my amazement she then asked me if I had given one to her good friend Nancy? I stated that I didn't know who Nancy was and she then said well, she's right over there. I then said well if she is your good friend then maybe you should give her one yourself, here is an extra one to do that.

I instructed her that you would also have to tell that is was a Gospel Tract and to read the back and answer the Good Person question. She again said thanks, and immediately walked over to her friend and gave it to her.

Later as Catherine and I were in line to give our condolences to the daughter of the deceased priest, another woman came up to me and stated the same thing the other lady said, why didn't you give me one? After I gave her the Million Dollar Gospel Tract, her husband took it from her, then I gave his wife another.

The husband appeared to be about my age, and while waiting in line, I was able to ask the questions about him being a good person using some of God's Ten Commandments. He admitted to breaking God's Law but he was saved because many years ago he walked forward at a Billy Graham event.

Afterwards Catherine told me that his wife who was standing there told her that she was so thankful that I had shared this message with him. It gave him a clear picture of how God has to punish those who have violated any of God's law and only by the repenting from those sins and placing our trust in the death and resurrection of Jesus Christ can we have eternally life. Not just because someone says a prayer or walks forward. She told Catherine that since his walk at Billy Graham's event, she has never seen any change in him.

So back to my original statement about the season for giving. What a wonderful gift to be able to share with ALL those we come in contact with, not just family and

friends. Even Catherine who was reluctant in the beginning has now become more faithful and excited about the responses she gets from those she gives them to. Just last night she gave out three. She is amazed when she tells them what it is, "a Gospel Tract and you need to answer the Million Dollar question, are you good enough to get into Heaven".

One lady after she was asked the question stated, "That question is more important than making a Million Dollars, I'll definitely read this when I get home!"

Catherine mentioned that she is so thankful that she has learned how to share the Glorious Gospel of the Lord and Savior Jesus the Christ, with those who are in the world. Now, even strangers, people you met every day can be approached!

When Christ told Peter, "come follow me and I will make you fishers of men". (Mark 1:17) I'm sure He wasn't telling Peter that it would only be to his family and friends that he was to share with and hopefully you understand that this command was not just for Peter. So now I can give a gift, a Million Dollar Gospel Tract, while becoming like fishers of men. This is the true message of what being born again is all about.

So, my friends I pray that you see this as a most wonderful GIFT, one that is remembered and desired by others, just like this funeral. We who are born again have been commanded and encouraged by our Lord and Savior as He stated in (Mark 16:15) and again in (Acts 1:8), to go out of your way to share with the lost. Now if you understand what our world is all about, "money", then why not give them what they want so they will have the opportunity to read the Word of God as well.

I pray you grasp the concept of using these Gospel Tracts, Million Dollar Bills. This is a way of reaching the lost simple, effectively and Biblically. Jesus Himself used the Ten Commandments in (Luke 18:18-25) Wouldn't be proper to honor Him to do the same? If you would like some of the Million Dollar Tracts let me know and I will gladly send some to you.

At this time, we wish you all a very Merry Christmas!

Attending other Churches

$\mathcal{B}$efore sharing the outcomes of other churches, I'd like to share what transpired at that mega church that I had attended for almost ten years.

Only by God's hand could this happen as I was asked to teach a class there on how to share the Gospel with Catholics. I say only God could have made this happen because I was not anyone who was teaching anything there, I had no degree of any kind.

A fellow brother in Christ, Alan Heflich, was my mentor as this man had been a follower of Jesus Christ for about twenty-five years and would help me understand the Scriptures. Well he was the I-T guy at the church and while attending one of the meetings about having teachers who could teach on how to witness to those of other religions. Alan found out that the man they had for teaching how to witness to those of the Catholic faith, couldn't make it and the classes were scheduled for the following week and they had no one that could do it. He told them about me and how I was raised a Catholic and could teach the group on how to do it. Can you imagine what it felt like when he called me and told me how I was appointed to teach the class. I was in awe, that I was being asked to teach at a mega church!

Now as awesome as this may sound, I have to give you the rest of the story, just like Paul Harvey said. Being this was my first-time teaching anything, I asked the lady in charge of all the classes if they could record me as I knew that had the equipment. Her 1st response was why did I want to be recorded as none of the other teachers asked to do that. I responded with well this is my 1st time and I would like to know what I sounded like so that I would be able to hear what I say and how I say it. Prayerfully I might be able to improve my teaching skills. She then agreed. I think you going to love this. The night before, the Lord gave me a way to get introduced. I had a black shirt and I took a white cardboard and cut it to fit around my neck. Now I looked like a priest. As I entered the classroom, I noticed that one of the walls was pulled and now two rooms were opened. WOW! There must have been about 75 people taking this class.

Being introduced by the leader, I looked around and realized many knew me so I then tore off the white carboard paper I had around my neck and announced that I was not a priest. You should have heard the ooh's and aah's, as those that did not know me actually thought tearing off my white piece was an abomination. That's when I asked, I noticed the reverence you showed me when you saw me dressed up as a priest, so how do you value me know? The place was silent. A few of them were glad that I wasn't a priest who would be teaching them.

I think I made my point to help them understand how Catholics give them reverence, instead of giving that reverence just to God. So on with the teaching as I had two Sunday sessions, the 1st Sunday I explained all the lies that have been taught over the centuries about, water Baptism, so called holy water, praying to Mary, and the fact that the Lord Jesus Christ Himself is brought down from Heaven when the priest gives them the holy Eucharist. The worst one is that the priest can give them absolution, right before they die and help them get into Heaven. If he does not, then that person is probably in Purgatory, which is not even mentioned in the Bible, Heaven or Hell, that's it.

Then on the 2nd Sunday I showed them how easy it would be if they used some of Ray Comfort's Gospel Tracts that ask them, "Are they good enough to get into Heaven". I read to them how the Bible in (Psalm 19:7), elaborates that by telling us that, It's the Law the converts the soul. In the New Testament even Paul says, "That the Law is a Schoolmaster to bring us to Christ by Faith." (Galatians 3:24) Sadly, many could not even name more than three! So, we went over them and I showed them how they could be easily internalized by the cartoon that Ray had made up showing each one as an icon next to what they stated.

After having them practice on each other taking turns holding out a Tract and asking a simple question, "Did you get one of these?" They seemed to understand how easy it would be to open up a conversation with a complete stranger or even one of their family members or friends. (Sometimes referred to as confrontation)

Sorry to go here but I think it must be told. The time is up and the person who is in charge of classes stands up in front of me and declares in an angry tone, "This is NOT how we do it here!" With that a lady across from her stood up and shouted out, 'WHY NOT, I never heard of anything like this and it makes a lot of sense?" The leader did not like that and they got into an argument over it. Needless to say, I was never asked to teach again.

Remember I asked the leader if they would record my teaching. Well come the next Sunday I asked her for the CD, she said she didn't have it. I then went to the person who I knew was recording it and he told me he left it on her keyboard that Sunday. Well here comes a blessing. About 3 months later I got a call from the leader who said she needed to ask for my forgiveness, as she had the CD all along, but didn't want me to have it because of how she was arguing with the lady at the class and that argument was on the CD. About a week later I received it in the mail with a written apology.

Praise the Lord for opening her eyes to her deception, but sadly speaking about God's Ten Commandments to those in church seems to be extremely offensive and something those in leadership frown upon.

In a Bible Study from the church I attended the women Pastor asked, "how do you show worshiping God? "I waited no one responded then I stated, that to me it was obedience by doing what He commanded that we should go and share with everyone. I stated that if it were possible and I didn't need sleep I would do it 7/24. With that a woman stated that she was new at this and hasn't shared with anyone, because it makes her uncomfortable to speak to others about her faith.

The pastor without hesitation told the lady that each of us has to find out what our gifts are, and not everyone is going to feel comfortable sharing with others. Very few have the gift of Evangelism! She then explained how the Bible states that we are all of the body, some have feet, some hands, some ears. (1Corinthians 12:4-10) But here Paul also states we have all the gifts! If (Philippians 4:13) is true, then could this baby Christian been told that possible through pray and petition the Lord could help her be one who could share with strangers, the gift of eternal life? (Romans 10:14-17)

Oh, BTW this is a class on prayer, you know how to commune with God. Then I guess we shouldn't be praying what Jesus himself asked of the Father in (Luke 10:2).

Anyone know it?

Here it is. And He was saying to them,

"The harvest is plentiful, but the laborers are few; therefore, beseech the Lord of the harvest to send out laborers into His harvest." (NASB)

Afterwards I went to another church where I knew of a Pastor who came from this church and didn't like it when I took one of his teens through the Commandments to see if he understood salvation.

When I asked this teen, did he know what Jesus did for him so that he wouldn't have to go to Hell? He said no, several times. I then told him what Jesus did, and he thanked me and said he never heard it like that before.

The Pastor's message on his Power Point presentation: If you love the Gospel, you will love to Evangelize! I couldn't believe what I was seeing! He stated how sad it is that our churches are no longer making it an important issue to reach the lost, they are more concerned about making those who come happy. He showed a survey from Barna Research that in;

2009 - 20 yrs. Ago

20% claimed to Evangelize

5 yrs. ago 4%

SADLY, Today **1%**

Maybe if this verse were as popular as (John 3:16), there would be a true revival. Then in (Luke 10:2), And He was saying to them, "The harvest is plentiful, but the laborers are few; therefore, beseech the Lord of the harvest to send out laborers into His harvest." Next Luke tells us what Jesus stated was true. Luke 24:42-49 These are My words which I spoke to you while I was still with you, that all things which are written about Me in the Law of Moses and the Prophets and the Psalms must be fulfilled. The Psalm that corresponds could be,

(Psalm 19:7). The law of the Lord is perfect, converting the soul;

1st Way of the Master Laboratory
April 2009

*P*raises to be given to our Lord and Savior Jesus the Christ!

Well, the first Way of the Master Laboratory seemed to be a great success!

Those who attended humbled themselves and admitted that they still had not approached anyone with what they had seen from the Way of The Master seminar they had attended. They still hadn't internalized the Ten Commandments nor were they comfortable about bringing them up in a conversation. This was time for all of us to pray, practice, participate, and prove ourselves with this method of using God's greatest weapon,

"The Ten Commandments!"

During the session those who participated continually repeated the questions that needs to be ask to help the unsaved to understand why they need a savior. It was stated several times how helpful it was to practice the concept of (W. D. J. D). (***What Did Jesus Do***).

I remembered being told that Confuses stated, "Repetition is the mother of learning." This is exactly what we did at this Laboratory. It was evident from this training how effective it was because of the confidence being shown after practicing with one another several times.

In the beginning of the training most of the participants couldn't recite the Commandments, but later they became more confident about saying them as well as their numbers, and how excited they became because of it.

I asked one of the men to come up front and then started to explain how sometimes I have seen men hiding behind a pole when they come with us to Tempe. Tempe Arizona is where the college, Arizona State University is located. Because of the large number who attend we have a great opportunity to Evangelize. It seemed like they were afraid to mingle with the crowd that forms on the sidewalk. He stated, "That would be me!" That he was literally petrified at being amongst a crowd of people to the point of almost passing out. At that point I asked his wife to come up so that he wouldn't be alone.

I mentioned that instead of hiding, that he come to another brother in Christ and ask that he pray for him and to take away the fear. We can only encourage one another if the one who is in need be transparent and confess the sin. What a blessing that would be to the one who could pray for him, and that way you would not be alone or isolated. Satan wants us to be alone and not show others our weakness. I can't be sure of this, but it looked like he was about to cry and so was his wife who was standing next to him.

I was pleasantly surprised at what happened next! I saw an amazing blessing from the Lord. Catherine was able to help me critique someone by stating what she hadn't heard them say as they were practicing. If any of you know Catherine, she is usually quiet. Now Catherine spoke up before I did, that was amazing to me. She spoke with such confidence that at first, I was shocked, but then well pleased. Catherine's comments were favorably accepted.

One of them didn't think it was advantageous to go to Tempe because he wanted to perfect his presentation. What a blessing to have the lady behind him state: "Okay, here I am practice on me!" While giving his presentation, I videotaped him and even though he stumbled he was able to get to the end.

This was a giant step because in the beginning

I was told by those who attend church,

"The public would NOT let me video tape them".

Everyone commented how well he did. He still wasn't satisfied because that when he is under pressure his mind goes blank. I mentioned to him that he was able to finish what he started which was a huge accomplishment and that he continues to practice. I think at that point it helped him understand that we don't have to be perfect to present this message, just be willing to do so. It seemed liked everyone's fear was waning because by listening to him stumble it helped them understand that it was okay not to be perfect.

After the training we shared some pizza and what was learned from the training. Everyone was thankful for getting together and appreciated what was discussed. All who came to the Laboratory also accompanied me to Tempe to watch, pray and maybe even speak.

All the glory was given to God because now present on a street in Tempe were more laborers for His Kingdom. (Luke 10:2) As I watched those who came to try out what they had learned I was thrilled to see some who had expressed anxiety before the training now engaging,

One-two-One, with the lost!

My pray coincides with (Luke 10:2), that more of you who have been through the Way of The Master Seminar now come to the Laboratory.

Bad day for Tom, Glorious day for the Lord

July 2009

$\mathcal{I}$ was leaving for Lake Havasu on Tuesday 7/21/09 for a few days to see some new prospects.

I had two appointments set up for that afternoon, so I needed to leave early in the morning.

I was late getting out of Phoenix and even missed the exit off of I-17 that would take me to Lake Havasu. This added an extra hour to my trip.

When I arrived at the motel, I misjudged the U-turn I was making and hit the curb hard. When I looked at the tire, I saw a gaping hole in it and what looked like a dent to the wheel. My first thought was about the expense of replacing the wheel, as I thought I could change the flat tire and continue on to my appointment. When I opened the trunk to get the spare and the jack, I couldn't find the jack handle.

I went inside the motel and asked the person if he had a jack handle that I could borrow. As he was getting it I went back to the car to remove the spare and found it to be flat. Fortunately, I have AAA, so I called them. They told me they would tow me to a tire place, and it would be about an hour wait. At this point I realized that I was not going to get to the two afternoon appointments I had, and became even more frustrated! That's when I started to pray, and asked the Lord what was it that I was to learn from this experience? I was asking, Why Me? I was very frustrated and losing my JOY!

The tow truck arrived and he said that I could sit in the cab while waiting for my car to be lifted onto the back of the truck. The guy from the motel came to the truck and offered me a bottle of water. As I opened the door I thought how thoughtful of him and it reminded me of what I'm called to be like, (James 1:2-3), as I thanked him I then gave him a Million Dollar Gospel Tract and told him to read the back.

Then it hit me that the Lord was using me to do His work and that the work that I had in mind was to be postponed. My demeanor changed as now I realized that I now would be witnessing to people that I would not have normally met. Besides giving out Million Dollar Gospel Tracts to the driver and a few of the workers at the tire store, I was able to share with a woman and her two sons who were waiting in the store, like me. This time I was able to spend more time about the message on the back and afterward the mom thanked me for sharing with her.

The next day I met with my new client from a few months ago to go over her new plan. I had given her a Million Dollar Gospel Tract when we first met a month ago and explained how I used it to share with others. She thanked me for sharing as she said she was also a Christian. I then gave her another one and asked her to give it to the next person she runs into.

When I finished explaining the benefits of her new plan, I told her what happened to me when I arrived in town, and how the Lord used me to share with strangers. She immediately asked that I not be offended and would I take back the Million Dollar Gospel Tract because she was not the outgoing type. I then asked her how outgoing does someone have to be to offer a Million Dollar Gospel Tract to someone who had just been kind enough to offer you a bottle of water?

At that point she became quiet and did not respond. Her trying to justify herself for not sharing now didn't make sense. I then asked her if she understood what Jesus Christ went through on the Cross? His punishment was brutal, severe, and painful. He did all that so that we would have a chance to be reconciled with God. Now that I belong to Him, how could I NOT hand someone a Gospel Tract who may not know what it means to be

"Born Again". How selfish is that! After a few more verses on what Christ commands of those He calls His own; (Mark 16:15, Acts 1:8).

She now started to understand that it's not about our personality or whether we are outgoing or not, but our obedience to the One who saved us. At this point I offered her a few more Million Dollar Gospel Tracts and asked if she would like to give it a try? She said she would and thanked me for sharing with her.

I guess by confronting her about her false belief, which seems in our culture today to be something horrific to do, the Lord opened her heart to see what a blessing it is to openly share with others. As I was leaving, she walked me to the door and stated, "The reason she bought the plan from me was because she trusted me.

Seminar and Open Air in Tempe

July 2009

We had a small attendance this time but there was one person who showed up that had a degree from Fuller Theological Seminary.

After the seminar some of them stated that they had not ever heard what they heard today as this was very helpful to help reach the lost.

One of the exciting moments for me was when I got a call from a man who had been to the training a few years ago and came again last month. He asked if I was going to Tempe after the seminar and that he would like to join me as he still hadn't been with me to Tempe. I told him I was. Could he come to the seminar around 4, so that he could share with the others what it was that he found it to be so difficult to reach out to those who are lost?

He agreed and when he came, he made it very clear how in all the years of being a Christian that he had never heard anyone using the Commandments as a way to share the Gospel with others. He mentioned that he was still struggling with reaching out to those he came in contact with but wanted to be an obedient servant for Christ. He realized that using the Ten Commandments to help them as to why they need a Savior made more sense to him now than ever before.

This was another awesome night as we had many sower's out there sharing the Gospel while handing out the Million Dollar Gospel Tracts that most people love to take.

My friend was excited that he was now able to reach out to perfect strangers and offer them these great "Ice Breakers, the Million Dollar Gospel Tract!" Now he experienced what happens when we asked them the question, "Are you good enough to get into Heaven", and how everyone was thankful that we took the time to share.

I read a story today about how someone asked a young girl about her religious beliefs. She told him that she just recently got baptized into the Mormon Church. He asked her why she did that and she stated that they were the only ones who spoke to her about her religious belief.

How sad was that! Those who are members of the Mormon Church go out of their way to share with others and thereby perpetuate their false doctrine to those who are still blind to the truth. How many people have crossed your path, and you choose to say nothing? Imagine how the One who gave His life for you must feel?

I've heard it said, "That what you believe is a personal matter, but it's not a private one!" (per Greg Laurie) So please join us when we have this training as I promise you will never be the same again.

One of the Exciting Moments

August 2009

One of the exciting moments for me was when I got a call from a man who had been to the training a few years ago and came again last month.

He asked if I was going to Tempe after the seminar and that he would like to join me as he still hadn't been with me to Tempe. I told him I was and could he come to the seminar around 4, so that he could share with the others what it was that he found it to be so difficult to reach out to those who are lost. He agreed and when he came, he made it very clear how in all the years of being a Christian that he had never heard anyone using the Commandments as a way to share the Gospel with others.

He mentioned that he was still struggling with reaching out to those he came in contact with but wanted to be an obedient servant for Christ. He realized that using the Ten Commandments to help them as to why they need a Savior made more sense to him now than ever before.

Watch this video, Tom asking Chris a prior catholic taking The Good Person Test. (about 4: mins into it) his girlfriend tries to pull him away and he doesn't go. Not knowing what God did for him so he wouldn't have to go to Hell, he answers that he honors his mother and father!

It was another awesome night as we had many sower's out there sharing the Gospel and handing out the Million Dollar Gospel Tracts that most people love to take.

My friend was excited that he was now able to reach out to perfect strangers and offer them these great "Ice Breakers, the Million Dollar Gospel Tracts ", and then experience what happens as we asked them the question, "Are you good enough to get into Heaven", and how everyone was thankful that we took the time to share.

Way of the Master Seminar

August 2009

This Saturday's seminar was certainly different! Why, well no one had signed up for it.

Now it's 11:30 that morning and I told Catherine that I was going there to see if anyone might show up. I remembered that when I first started doing this that Catherine asked me, "What if only one person signed up would I still do the training?" I thought about that and then realized this wasn't about me or how many, but what the Lord wanted all of us who are Born Again to do, "Go share the Gospel." (Mark 16:15)

I was sitting at my desk not really expecting anyone, I didn't even put out the welcome sign that I had put out for the last four years. I heard a knock on the door and behold there were two women standing there who asked if this is where the Way of the Master Seminar was being held? Needless to say, I was quite pleasantly surprised as I recognized that the Lord had sent me two potential laborers.

I asked how they heard about it, as all my invites require letting me know whether or not they are attending. They told me it was from some Women's Organization in East Mesa and that one of their members said she had been and suggested that they attend. One came all the way from Chandler.

This was the first time that I had only two attendees. I was able to answer more of their questions and hear more about them personally. One had been trained in the Evangelism Explosion method when she was in her teens. She was very impressed on how easy it was to hand out the unique Tracts and to ask them about being a "Good Person". She had never heard about how Jesus Himself used the Commandments to show the unrighteous what standard God required to enter Heaven (Mathew 5:28), (Mark 10:17), (Luke 18:20) to name a few.

The major topic that always comes up is, "***confrontation***". I made this big and bold because it seems to be one of the biggest stumbling blocks, beside personal fear of not knowing enough when sharing. I asked what thoughts come to mind when they hear this word. Now, is it positive or negative? One of them quickly stated negative and the other thought for a moment and stated it could be positive but mostly negative. I then share what I found in the dictionary as one of the meanings, that "it's an attempt to reconcile!"

Maybe if we focus on this definition, then we wouldn't have much trouble sharing with the lost. Why? Because, by giving them the truth, the whole truth, which would help them see that they are Law breakers and deserve to be punished, then give them the Good News, it would make more sense.

I'm sure you would agree that time does not forgive sin. We should be careful about sharing with those we love and NOT be providing them with half the truth, that all they need is just to accept Jesus! This is what the Lord Himself stated:

Many will say to Me on that day, 'Lord, Lord, did we not prophesy in Your name, and in Your name cast out demons, and in Your name perform many miracles?' 23 And then I will declare to them, 'I never knew you; depart from Me, you who practice lawlessness.' (Matthew 7:22-23)

Many of you know that the goal of the seminar, crash course, whatever you want to call it, it's to help those who come to confront their fears and Trust in Jesus. I can do all things through Christ who strengthens me. (Phil 4:13)

I mentioned to them that I was going to Tempe to show them how we share with strangers, but they didn't know about that and had other plans, so they didn't come. It's truly amazing how almost any message I have heard about sharing with others, they almost always never mention sharing with strangers. Its family, co-workers, and friends. I don't know about you but I don't have 50 family members or friends or co-workers that I could share with. Since learning Ray Comfort's message from the Way of The Master in 2004, I have encountered thousands of strangers over the last five years who have either been given a Gospel Tract and/or answered how God would see them using the Ten Commandments.

While I was on Mill Ave in Tempe, a young man on a skate board came by us and asked, "Were we with the same people he had seen before who hand out Million Dollar Gospel Tracts?" My good friend Al responded by asking the young man if he had ever answered the questions on the back of the bill, and would he like to answer them now?

I hope you understand that this is NOT the magic words that make someone a follower of Christ but it does help them understand why they need Jesus to save them from Hell.

My prayer goes out to all who claim Christ as Lord and Savior, too understand that as true followers we emulate what our Lord did. Jesus said He came to save the lost! Why is it we only think that our family, co-workers and friends are those who are lost? Please think about all of the strangers the Lord has placed in your path and because of your fear, (you fill in what kind you have) with one of them being, **to confront**.

We allow the world (which if I understand scripture is controlled by Satan) to dictate how we are to behave as Satan requires with one another. Being filled with the Holy Spirit tells our hearts we know that many are headed for a most unimaginable destiny...

ETERNAL PUNISHMENT IN HELL!

We typically say nothing to warn them!

This one concerned me!

When I say to the wicked, 'O wicked man, you will surely die,' and you do not speak to warn the wicked from his way, that wicked man shall die in his iniquity, but his blood I will require from your hand. 9 But if you on your part warn a wicked man to turn from his way and he does not turn from his way, he will die in his iniquity, but you have delivered your life. (Ezekiel 33:8-9)

By using these Tracts as "ice breakers" I have been able to confront and share with thousands of people over the last fifteen years and can't remember any stranger being offended.

Way of the Master at Fathers Fellowship
October 2009

Today I was truly blessed, as the Pastor from The Father's Fellowship Church asked me to host The Way of the Master Seminar at his Church!

I just started going this Church about a month ago. They had just started the series from the weekly training for their Tuesday evening Bible study and I started to attend.

It was the second time I was there and Pastor Jack took me outside before the meeting and asked if I would put on the 1/2-day seminar for his people as I had been sharing with him that I had been doing The Way of the Master Seminars for the last four years. It was exciting to hear him announce that on Sunday, that this Saturday I would be hosting this seminar and that all should attend.

I stood by the sign-up table after the worship service prayerfully hoping that some would sign up. The Lord definitely touched the hearts of those who were there as several signed up for the training.

The day came and the training was well received. There were many somber and humorous moments. Somber, because when they viewed the video that showed a group of teenagers who couldn't name any of the Ten Commandments,

(Romans 2:15) but had no problem naming 10 different brands of beer. The humor when they heard some of the ridiculous answers from those who were taking the "Good Person Test" (Galatians 3:24)

It was a blessing to have others who had been through this before come just to share what listening to this teaching had done for them. One of the ladies named Ann lives about 45 minutes away and shared how this training changed how she shares, as she admitted being a Christian for at least 50 years and never used the Law to help anyone to understand why they need a Savior.

Dan, another brother in Christ, who was not a member of this church but came to the seminar because he had been out on the streets with us and he wanted to encourage the group to at least come out on the streets to see us in action. This is what helped him understand how using Tracts and the Law was an easy way to share and it gave him a desire to want to reach out to save those who are lost. (Acts 1:8)

Well the five hours passed quickly as now it was time for prayer and nourishment. Some came with me to Tempe to observe how this actually works with strangers. While standing on a box I draw a crowd by giving away money, by asking trivial questions. At the right time I ask, "Who here can prove to me that they are a Good Person?" Someone's hand always goes up! (1Tim. 1:8)

One of the ladies, named Ella, (who has beautiful white hair) came from the seminar. This was her first Way of the Master Seminar and she came down with me as she doesn't like driving at night. She was on fire as she handed out several Million Dollar Gospel Tracts to perfect strangers. All her life she said she has wanted to share, but never did anything like this. She mentioned to me that she was going to call and order her own pack of Million Dollar Gospel Tracts so that she can give them away wherever she goes.

Then there was Andres and his 13-year-old son. It was amazing to watch how this young boy on his own requested to have some of the Million Dollar Gospel Tracts so that he could hand them out like we were. (Mat. 18:3)

Well, today was a long day as we got finished around 10:30 PM. Lots of Tracts were handed out and many one-two-ones were done. We praise the Lord for giving us the passion and desire to go out to reach and save the lost.

We are nobody's who can share with everybody about somebody who can save anybody. (Mark 16:15)

Here are (2) comments from one who came twice.

*T*om, when I first heard about The Way of the Master Method, I was a little hesitant because I tend to be very reserved, especially to people I don't know.

As I've grown with the Lord, He has given me compassion for people that I've never had before. My problem was that I couldn't find the "right" time and that I was too fearful of what they might say/think of me.

As I watched the video's it really struck me how many people thought they were going to Heaven just because they believe they're a good person. So many people are deceived and NEED the truth told to them. I realized that I can't ultimately change these lost souls, but I need to do my part as a Christian to spread the love of Jesus Christ. This series has made me more knowledgeable in how to teach others about the Ten Commandments and how God is not only a God of love, but a God of justice. We all need to ask our Heavenly Father for forgiveness of our sins and make Him our guide in everything we do.

These Tracts are perfect icebreakers that really enforce individuals to think about the ultimate question: "Am I good enough to go to Heaven?" After watching Kirk Cameron, Ray Comfort, and you talk to random people on the street I could see how they were really pondering their status with God and very thankful for taking the time to reach out to them.

That would be so awesome if I could also be that person to lead someone to Jesus. The Way of the Master has changed my life in recognizing the value of people's salvation and giving me the confidence to lead them to ultimate fulfillment.

Thank you for all that you do in glorifying our Lord.
Sincerely,

Christa

Here is her 2nd comment

Tom,

I want to say thanks again for everything you've done. It was such a learning experience for me. I will never forget my first time out there. I will for sure do it again!
Have a blessed week.
Christa

You notice that this time Christa came with us after the seminar to Tempe. My understanding on what I mostly hear preached, is that we are to share with our family, friends and co-workers. Jesus didn't just talk to that group, if He did then only a select group would have been saved.

So how many times can we tell those people why they need to have Jesus? It won't make sense to those who think they have done nothing wrong. (1st Cor. 1:18) Just because their life is not going like they would like it, you know having a great job, making more money, better relationships, a happier marriage, if they just accept Jesus He will fix all of that. This is the NOT why He came. Read (Mat 9:13, Mark 2:17, Luke 5:32,) to understand why from His own words. He didn't come to go through such an agonizing death just so you could have a better life! He came because of our sinfulness. If we're not being faithful servants and warning others about the horrible consequence of sin,(Romans 6:23) then we are spreading a different Gospel.

In (Luke 18:18)Jesus gave us a way to show those who claim to be righteous, how they need to humble themselves and acknowledge that have violated God's Law. When they understand this fact, they can understand why they need to repent and place their trust in Jesus Christ alone!

This teaching from Ray Comfort and Kirk Cameron, "The Way of the Master", helps us do just that. Some of you know that it starts out by asking everyone if they consider themselves to be a "Good Person". Most state they are! *"Most men will proclaim everyone his own goodness: but a faithful man who can find?* (Proverbs 20:6.)

Then after asking permission if they would like to test it to see if it's true, we then can ask them some of the Ten Commandments. Most Christians I've meet don't know them, do you? Then if they have ever broken any of them, just like Jesus questioned the rich young ruler, in (Luke 18:18). Aren't we supposed to be following Jesus, so wouldn't you think, saying what He said would be pleasing to him?

This teaching will encourage you, convict you, and by the Holy Spirit transform you into a laborer for the Lord, just like His prayer in (Luke 10:2).

Here is a quote from Charles Spurgeon:

"I do not believe that any man can preach the gospel who does not preach Law. The Law is the needle, and you cannot draw the silken tread of the gospel through a man's heart until you first send the Law to make way for it."

My prayer is that when this teaching is being held again that you prayerfully ask yourself why you wouldn't want to be one of His, to do what the Lord asks of you, as we are all His children and if we say we love Him, then He tells us what He expects from us in,

(John 14:21, Mark 16:15), as well as in (Acts 1:8).

Just Another Lunch at Mongolian Barbecue

November 2009

This Monday I had lunch at the Mongolian Barbecue restaurant with Pastor Blace, in Scottsdale. After the cashier told how much it was, I offered her the Million Dollar Gospel Tract and asked if she could make change?

She laughed and said, "Yea right!" I told her when she went home that she should read the back as it had the Million Dollar question on it, "Are you good enough to get into Heaven?"

At this place you fill your own bowl, and place it on a counter where one of the cooks throws the food onto a very, very, large flat hot plate, and it simmers. I saw the Pastor place a dollar bill into a fishbowl and did the same but added a Million Dollar Gospel tract with it. That's when the lady in front of the Pastor made a comment about the Million Dollars and he turned to me to tell me she was curious about it. I then gave him one and told him to give it to her and to be sure to tell her to read the back.

Now the cooks saw the Million Dollar Gospel Tract in the fishbowl and commented that they would be very rich. I then asked one of the cooks how many cooks are working here and he stated that there were five. I then counted out five Million Dollar Gospel tracts and placed them into the fishbowl. I then told them that they have to read the back of the bill because you can't get any change from these bills because they don't make a Million Dollar bill, but it can change their lives if they read it. Is this what Paul had in mind when telling us to be ready in season and out of season! In other word always!

Remember (2Timothy 4:1-5)

Now comes the best part that I thank God for. Blace, my friend, just as we were finishing up our meal, the cashier Maria came to me because she wanted to talk to me about what the back of the bill said.

As I walked her through the Law, asking if she had ever lied, stolen or as Jesus said, "If you just look at a person with lust, you have already committed adultery with them in your heart." That's in Mat. 5:28. She tried to justify her sin's against God and that God was a loving God and all she had to do was confess her sins to a priest and God would forgive her. (sound familiar?)

I then explained to her if I had violated her sister and got caught and was now standing before the Judge and then confessed what I had done to her sister and then said, "I was sorry", would he let me go? She looked at me with a new face and said, "NO!" I then asked her how could a Holy, Righteous, and Just God do any less?

Now when I asked her how would God find her based on what she just admitted? She then stated she would be guilty, and God would have to send her to Hell. I then asked her if it concerned her that she could be in Hell, and she said "YES!" I could now see a changed look on her face as it seemed it really bother her. Believing that would be her destination.

I asked her if you knew what Hell was like? She said she never heard her church talk about it. I explained it's where your thirst is never quenched, constant gnashing of teeth and worms never die, being tormented for eternity in the lake of fire. I then asked her if she knew what God did for her so she wouldn't have to go to Hell and she said, "NO." You can find that in Matthew 13:42,50

Then I asked her a 2nd time and this time she stated that Jesus Died on the cross. With that I then said does that mean that everyone who has heard that Jesus died on the cross is going to Heaven? So, all liars, thieves, murderers, or pedophiles are all going to be in Heaven? This time she became very somber and stated that wouldn't make sense!

I then explained to her that the only way we can be set free from our sins is to REPENT! This means to have remorse, regret with genuine sorrow, knowing that we have offended a Holy God, and that we deserve Hell. We need to turn away from sin and place our TRUST in Jesus Christ ALONE.

The Bible states that when we do this we are now, (please write these three down)

- "Born Again", (John 3:3).
- Then, "The old is gone the new has come." (2Cor. 5:17)
- It's Godly sorry that produces REPENTANCE, that leads to Salvation! (2Cor. 7:10)

And when Maria heard that she stated,

"Now I understand what you're saying!"

As we were leaving my Pastor wanted to treat me to some ice cream, but I declined. But when I saw what Maria brought, I told Maria I changed my mind and would like to buy one. She came back with my ice cream and told me, I think your you're gonna love this… "it was a gift from her to me".

What happened next surprised me as Pastor Blace, who rejects using this method of sharing the Gospel, stretched out his hand and stated that was awesome! Then he added, but it's not my thing.

So why should you give out tracts?
Here are 10 reasons:

1. They are a very economical form of evangelism
2. They work while we sleep
3. They have the ability to get into a house and stay there
4. They are never afraid or show cowardice
5. They are never tempted to compromise their message
6. They never get tired, discouraged or give up
7. They stick to what they have to say and never argue
8. They can present the message when we don't have time
9. They can go to places where we cannot
10. When they are read, they get people in the mood – and then you could speak to them

When giving out tracts don't ask, "Would you like one of these?" They will probably just say "No", or "What is it?" Instead ask,

"Did you get one of these?" That makes the person feel that he is missing out on something, and it also stirs up curiosity.

Try it…it really works!

My Surgery, at the Hospital
December 2009

Catherine brought me to the hospital around 9:30AM.

The reason for checking into the hospital, is because my Doctor diagnosed that my shin had evidence of a Melanoma cancer.

As I approached the receptionist, she got a Million-Dollar Bill. The next check in lady got a Million-dollar bill as well. These two were in close proximity so as I was leaving, I asked if they liked illusions? Both sad yes so, I showed them the Red and Blue illusion cards and gave one to each of them.

A nurse's aide came and escorted me to the pre-op with another patient, yep they both got a Million. Much to my pleasant surprise my good friend Pastor Blace was there waiting for me in the pre-opt check-in. Nice to have a Brother with you when you're facing surgery.

A nurse escorted me to my bed and she was rewarded with one as well. She liked it so much I asked if she would like to have more to hand out to those she knew and excitedly she took a bunch. Now only wearing the gown I placed all my Tracts on the bed. Catherine was with me and she had some in her purse as well. She was also handing them out to anyone she came in contact with.

I was now being wheeled to my first test before surgery on my leg for the melanoma cancer on my shin. Another assistant came to help and "yep!" She got one as well for being a safe driver.

In the room the male nurse who got me ready on the screening table got his Million-dollar reward for being gentle. The doctor came in to give me my nuclear shot, so they could see where the cancer was traveling.

Before he injected me, I asked if I gave him a Million Dollars would he be gentile with me? (He said yes, so he got one)

He gently explained how this procedure helped the surgeon, and asked if I had any questions. Still lying on the table, I told him that on the back of the Million-Dollar bill was a question that needed an answer, "Are you good enough to get into Heaven? Much to my surprise he stood there and I walked him through the commandments. When we got to the question, "Heaven or Hell", because he admitted breaking all the commandments, he stated that he didn't believe in Hell.

I mentioned to him that if I didn't believe I had cancer it wouldn't mean that it was true. The Bible makes it very clear, that Hell exists. If it did, based on what we discussed, where would you go? Now the look on his face changed from being confident to that look of uncertainty. He never answered, but thanked me for my sharing and said he would read the back of the bill later.

Another aid came to wheel me back to my waiting area, and I offered her a Million Dollar Gospel Tract and then she asked, "If this was one that had President Reagan on it?" Wondering how she knew, I said yes, and she told me her friend had given her one. I then asked if she had any friends and would like to have a few so she can give them to her friends. She said sure, and thanked me!

Now back in my pre-op room, I tried to get more comfortable in my bed and knocked all the tracks to the floor. At that moment a nurse passed by and stated, "here let me get that for you", and then said, "oh my God! those are Million Dollar Gospel Tracts!" I explained how they were not real but had a very important message on them and I use them to share with everyone I meet. She thought that was thoughtful as sometimes we need to be sharing with others. As she continued speaking, I noticed her demeanor starting to change, as her eyes seemed to look sad. I asked if she was okay and she started to share with me that her husband was leaving her after they had been married for over 18 years. I asked if I could pray for her and she said yes, thank you.

Another pleasant surprise was my Pastor Jack showed up around 1 pm and stayed with Catherine after they took me into surgery around 3:45PM. The nurse who came by to set me up with an IV, yep, she got one too.

Then the anesthesiologist came to my bed to explain his role and I asked him what would happen if I didn't wake up from the surgery, where would I go? I was able to share with him about our final destination and then asked him what would happen to him if he didn't wake up from a sleep. You know the rest of the story.

Though I must say my biggest surprise was when one of the women from Jack's Church, Laura, came around 3PM. She now wanted to comfort Catherine while I would be in surgery. She was there to help me out of the hospital around 7:30PM. I thank the Lord for Laura's heart to give up her time to be with Catherine during that time.

Some of you might be saying I don't hear about anyone accepting Jesus as Lord and Savior. Well I believe our job as one who has been born again, adopted into His Glorious Kingdom, are called to plant the seeds of truth, not just Grace... and tell them to say a prayer.

The truth comes first, so that they will understand why they need our Savior. Each one of us has violated God's commandments and deserves Hell, but most of us are not told about the Wrath of God and how His standards are far above ours. Once a person understands they are guilty, God can open their eyes so that they can understand that the only way for all of their sins to be washed away, is if they repent, and place their trust in Jesus Christ alone! That's probably why Jesus gave the rich young ruler five of the Ten Commandments when the Rich Young ruler asked, "What must I do to have eternal life?" (Luke 18:18-20)

I hope some of the Pastor's read this and glean from it as this is something that those who attend your worship service can learn this teaching using these unique tracks to hand out to perfect strangers. Can you imagine the army that would be raised up for the Lord! He would have more warriors reaching out to those less fortunate souls who may never come into a Church. Remember what Paul said in (1st Cor. 2: 1-4)

I mention this with a humble heart knowing that more of us can have similar encounters if only we place our trust in Him. (Phil. 4:13) I would love to have any comments you may have on why using this method of sharing is not Biblical, as I do not want to be doing the work of Satan. But if it is, then shouldn't it be offered to those who come to Worship?

Again, Catherine and I want to thank all of you for your prayers during this time. I thank the Lord for His mercy and discernment about this method of sharing the truth with everyone we meet.

Now we can say that, "we are nobodies who can share with everybody about somebody who can save anybody"

Saturday at Pat's Pizza January 2010

I want to make this perfectly clear that this story is NOT about me, but about how anyone of us who claims Christ as Lord can experience the same kind of interaction.

(Proverbs 11:30)

I met with my good friend Blace at Pat's Pizza, where God allowed me to show him exactly how to open a conversation with perfect strangers. We were discussing how the Lord expects us to share what we have received with others who may be lost. (Mark 16:15, Acts 1:8, Acts 10:42) He then commented on the verse in (Eze. 3:18-19), that those who we do not warn, their blood will be on our hands, but if we warn them and they don't listen then are hands are clean. I agreed with him and just as we were ready to leave, I asked him did he know of anyone who would try to share with the two ladies sitting on the other side of the restaurant. He sheepishly responded that he didn't, and probably wouldn't do it either.

Just then, several teenage boys came in followed by several other teens. Now the line went from the ordering counter back to the entrance, probably 15 to 20 teens. As I stood up to leave, I noticed that one was smiling and asked if he wanted to see something funny? I snapped my fingers and pointed a Blace's ear and a silver coin appeared that has Ten Commandments on one side and the Gospel of Jesus Christ on the other side. The young man was amazed! Then I showed how the coin can come out of Blace's ear to another teen. Now they wanted to know how to do it. Now standing, as most of them were now seated, I mentioned that it was an illusion and asked them if they would like to see another one. I took out the Red and Blue illusion cards, which are the same size and asked them which color looks bigger to them. Now about ten of them were watching and stating, Red, Blue, Red, as I moved the cards from left to right, stating how can that be when I've shown you that they are the same size?

This gave me the opportunity to ask them about the Ten Commandments and as I started asking the first question using the ninth commandment, have you ever told a lie? With that one young man admitted it, with a big grin. I focused on him when I asked the next three commandments, the 8th, 3rd and 7th, I asked base on just those four which he admitted to breaking, he stated he was guilty. I asked how would God find him, innocent or guilty? He stated that he would be guilty in front of a Holy God.

I then I asked where would God have to send him, Heaven or Hell? He stated HELL! I asked if this concerned him, and he thought for a while and then he arrogantly, said NO! I then asked if he knew what Hell was like and he replied no. I then explained to him what Jesus said it was like. Your thirst never quenched, (Arizona 126 degrees, Hell 1,226 degrees), constant gnashing of teeth, and where worms never die, being eaten alive for eternity! His attitude changed when I now asked him if it concerned him, and he said, "YES!"

I then asked if he knew what God had done so that he wouldn't have to go to Hell? After a long pause he said no, and the other teen sitting with him said, we've been forgiven? I then asked does that mean that all of us are going to be in Heaven, LIARS, THIEVES, FORNICATORS, and he responded with a NO!

Now everyone in the restaurant was listening so I gave the example of being guilty in front of a judge and telling the judge I was sorry please forgive me so that the judge would let me go, and they all agreed that a good judge would not do that. I could see the one young man on my right looking a lot more serious than before. I then explained what God had done for us. He sent His only Begotten Son to die on the cross to pay the price for the sins that I had committed. It's like being guilty, standing in front of that judge, now if someone was willing to pay the fine, or do the time, take the punishment for what I've done, then the judge can let me go.

That's what Jesus did for those of us who know that they are guilty of breaking God's Law and deserve Hell. Jesus took the horrible punishment that I deserved, the beating, mocking and being crucified as the perfect sacrifice so that if I REPENT, have remorse, regret, for what I've caused Him to have to go through, and now place my trust in Jesus Christ alone, then my sins will be forgiven, past, present, future.

I then passed out at least twenty more Million Dollar Gospel Tracts to everyone in the restaurant and thanked them for listening to me and that they needed to read the back of it because it has the most important question and answer..."Are you good enough to get into Heaven!" Why use the Law, the Bible tells us so? (1Timothy 1:8-11)

Now comes the most amazing part as the Pastor was still there with me as I thought he had left. Outside he put his arms around me and stated, "That was awesome!"

I thanked him and then said to him,

" This, you can do as well!"

(Mark 16:15, Acts 1:8)

My Poem, Who Am I?

Written January 2010
Does this REFLECT You?

Who am I If I'm not me?
Who am I since God changed me?

In **John 3: 3 Jesus** tells me

being born again is what I need to be.

Who am I If I'm not me?
Who am I since God changed me?

I thank God as I tell everyone I see
I 'm like that cause **Psalm 19:7** converted me.

The Laws I broke so many times
Jesus paid my debt by paying my fine.

Who am I If I'm not me?
Who am I since God changed me?

Mark 16-15 He commands me to go,
So, I can tell the world, before I go.

I share with all I meet with intent

so they would know they need to **REPENT**.

In **Acts 1:8 Jesus** ascended on High

all my sins **He** took that's when **He** said bye.

I know **He** wanted to give me a lift
I'd receive the Holy Spirit and that is my gift.

Who am I If I'm not me?
Who am I since God changed me?

In **Galatians 3:24**, Paul reminds us why the Law.
This teacher, tutor, schoolmaster shows me all. Unless I admit my sins to all, it would not please **Him** at all.

Unless I **REPENT** and trust in **Him**,
I could not be one who could follow **Him.**

Who am I If I'm not me.?
Who am I since God changed me?

Ephesians 2:8 and **9** Paul

states **His** Grace is what I needed
without it I never could have succeeded.

To show my love for **Him** in **John 14:15** as **He** requires,
I now do as **He** commands because it's my desire.

Who am I'm if I'm not me?

Ephesians 1:5 Paul tells me I'm an

adopted child, into the Kingdom of Heaven,
where forever I will be.

Would like to know if you've been adopted into the Kingdom?

It's as easy as 1-2-3
1 John, Chapter 2 verse 3 and of course read the rest of it
written by Thomas L. Fusco
For more about this go to my website:
www.tillthenetsRFull.org

Attorney Joe C. Men's Breakfast Meeting

January 2010

*T*hanks for all your prayers and support. I was blessed to have two of my brothers in Christ, Al and Dale with me to help engage with these men after the breakfast. With the five minutes I was given I emphasized why those who claim Jesus the Christ as Lord are commanded to share with the lost, not just friends and family as is the more acceptable tradition. In (Acts 10:42), Paul stated" And he commanded us to preach unto the people, and to testify that it is He which was ordained of God to be the Judge of quick and dead." (Know any pew sitters?)
(John 14:21,Mark 16:15, Acts 1:8)

One of the comments I shared with these men was what the Lord had given me early one morning. JFK's famous quote,

"Ask not what your country can do for you, but ask what you can do for your country!"
What we should be asking is,
"Ask not what Jesus can do for you, but what you can do for Jesus!"

I then mentioned to these men what seems to be really difficult is to start a conversation with a perfect stranger. Maybe you don't really care what happens to that stranger, it's not your job, or maybe someone will become his friend who goes to a church and then that pastor can save him. If this was them then they should read(2nd Cor. 13:5) If you really appreciated what our Lord and Savior Jesus the Christ did for you on that cross, you would be out shouting in the streets, so that everyone knew what an unbelievable gift you had received.

To quote Charles Spurgeon:

"We must school and train ourselves to deal personal with the unconverted. We must not excuse ourselves, but force ourselves to the irksome task until it becomes easy."

Because of taking the Training and Practicing it, makes it easy. The most common objections I hear for not sharing is, I'm a quiet person, I don't like to speak with other people, I've been told to wait for God to tell me when to speak to someone, the final one is, I don't feel comfortable speaking to a perfect stranger about my faith as they could ask me a question that I don't know. (So why not be honest and say you don't know and then find out!)

Remember, He calls whom He equips, not those who are equipped. To many of us say we follow Jesus but only if He is our co-pilot!

I asked some of the pastors if this concept of reaching the lost could be taught at their place. The response was almost the same. They had their own way and they didn't think that scattering Tracts was of much use because you wouldn't be able to come alongside a person or bring them into the Church where his teaching would save them. They said they were only interested in bringing someone into their church, so that through their message they could make them a Christian. Once that happened, then that person could go out and bring in another person, and so on.

I was told that it was a waste of time to just hand out Tracts and speak to strangers who I may never see again. This is because they may never come to our church where we would be able to teach them further in the Word. These people need to have a close relationship with the person sharing. But they were thankful that God had given me the gift to Evangelize to those people, but they were satisfied that what they were doing was what God had in mind for them to do. I even had one claim he would speak only to those

God told him to speak to and he repeated that comment several times, so that I wouldn't ask him if he would like to learn how to share with everyone.

Then Al commented about a pastor who was sitting next to him. (with the cross around his neck) This man was so against everything we tried to say really bothered him. Not the man himself, but that reaction from a pastor. I let him off easy and just moved on to talk to others, but maybe we should be a little more aggressive towards a pastor. They will be judged more harshly, according to Scripture. He's either deceived or a deceiver and it doesn't really matter which one.

They seemed to think that they are making the conversion; they're building their church, puffing themselves up. I should have asked him, "What caused Satan's fall?" Selfish pride caused it, and the Bible tells us that pride comes before a fall. If one thinks that scattering Gospel seed is useless, that man obviously thinks that he has the secret to bringing people to salvation, through his own works. God's Word does not return void, and who are these mere mortals to speak of God's Word with such derision in their voice?

Anyway, there were people who were open to the idea, excited by the Tracts, and a few of them even asked for extra Tracts to give to friends and family. Al then mentioned how he liked what the guy who'd been in prison said. He said, "There was going to be a change this year, and people weren't going to like it. No more sitting around being nice, we are to get out there and tell the Truth, whether anyone likes it or not!"

Now the good news! Well a few men came to me and admitted that they did not speak to others about what God had done for them because they were shy and mostly kept to themselves. These were humble men, not using the excuse that so many Christians use so then can justify their neglect and lack of love for what Christ has done for them. They knew they should share but were uncomfortable to even try. When I asked them could they ask a perfect stranger, "did you get your first Million yet," they said yes, they could, so I encouraged them to sign up for the Crash Course I was leading, and watch the Lord perform a miracle.

Some asked if we had any extra Million Dollar Gospel Tracts, so that they could hand out some as well. I was encouraged by the woman who was serving us the food, as this was for men only. I gave her one for serving such a delicious breakfast and then asked her the Million Dollar question, "Are you Good enough to get to Heaven" She said yes. Then I read the back of the bill with her and then she understood that she wasn't and said, "WOW! This is awesome! I like how easy this is to explain.

She then said, "I'm a Christian do you have any extra as I would love to give them to some people I know." I then gave her a bunch and then explained that if she would come to this Crash Course, I would show her how she could not only give it to her friends but everyone she comes in contact with. If that were true, how much more effective as a Christian do you think you would be? (You should have seen the look on her face, like a light bulb just turned on)

Well it's a good thing that our Lord and Savior wasn't like this. Can you imagine what He was thinking when He went with His disciples to Gethsemane and was praying, sweating blood, because He knew what He was going to go through the next day?

- Judas would betray Him
- His disciples would abandon Him
- Falsely accused in a mock trial
- He would be beaten, punched in the face, whipped, spit on mocked, striped of His clothes
- Rejected by His own people
- Sentenced to a horrendous death by carrying a heavy wooden cross, wearing a crown of thorns and then be nailed to it and hang there for about three hours all the while taking on the sins of the world.

- This part had to be the most painful punishment as this Man Jesus, who was God in human form, never knowing sin, now taking on the sins of the world to satisfy the only sacrifice acceptable to our Heavenly Father. Then came the worst and most agonizing torture of all…when he stated, "Father why has thou forsaken me." Here we see Jesus all alone as our Father in Heaven turned away from the only Begotten Son. Jesus was looking for a plan "B" but did the will of the Father, can't we!

(Matt. 26:29, Luke 22:24, Mark 14:36)

Shouldn't we overcome our fear by placing our trust Him alone?

Sharing with everyone with meet, not just friends and family? (Phil 4:13)

Of course, those of us who have been chosen and are adopted into the Kingdom understand that this was God's plan of redemption for mankind and His death brought us life as He was raised from the dead three days later.

We now know we have the gift of eternal life because of what happened then, and those of us who place our trust in what He did that day and repent from our own selfish desires will spend eternity with Him in Heaven.

How then can anyone who claims Him as Lord not have the desire to do as He commanded to GO into the ALL the world and proclaim the Gospel to ALL creation. (Mark 16:15)

Well the final blessing was when Al brought a man to me who asked if I would like to use his Tour Bus as a place to have my Crash Course. He explained that the bus takes them out for about four hours, each seat has its own TV monitor. They can be driven to a place like Prescott and while they are confined in the bus (can't leave, ha, ha) they can be trained on how to reach the lost and then when in Prescott practice handing out and sharing with those we meet there. I asked how much would it cost and he replied that the Lord would provide!

WOW, to say the least, I was shocked!

I pray that those of you have not been able to communicate this message that our Lord suffered so much for to come to this Crash Course.

Remember what Spurgeon stated earlier well he also stated this as well: "If you're not seeking to save the lost then you're not saved yourself, you can be sure of that!"

And of course we must honor our Lord when He prayed in (Luke 10:2)

And He was saying to them, "The harvest is plentiful, but the laborers are few; therefore, beseech the Lord of the harvest to send out laborers into His harvest."

So, if you're still struggling with reaching out to others, need some practice, I pray you come to the next Crash Course. (no more excuses!)

Today Honoring the Lord at McDonald's

Glory to God! July 2010

I just had to post this today, as it truly was for the Glory of our Lord and Savior Jesus Christ!

I was able to give out twenty Gospel Tracts and had many "One-two-One Encounters". It started out at McDonald's around 7AM where I meet with two men to study God's Word and hold each other accountable for our actions.

A little girl came walking by our table with a very pretty doll with thick blond hair. I commented on the doll's hair and saw a big smile on the girl's face. I asked how old she was and she said nine yrs. old. She turned to sit with what looked like her grandfather and I asked him if I could show his granddaughter a trick. He nodded and I made the Ten Commandment coin appear out of thin air. Her eyes got really big and she asked how I did that.

Now what happens next is not unusual as this is the reaction I usually get. Her hand reached out for it as if it belonged to her. I then asked if she would like to have it, she said yes. I then told her that it was a commemorative coin and that it had the Ten Commandments on one side and the Gospel of Jesus Christ on the other and to have her grandfather read it to her. (If any of you know me, you know that I have a hearing problem and I'm sure that others heard me)

The next part is also typical because she had two sisters who saw her get something and they then had their hands out as well. I gave them each a coin and then gave the first one three of the Million Dollar Gospel Tracts and asked if she would give them to her grandfather and her parents who were sitting at the next table. The grandfather read the back and thanked us for sharing!

Next my Brother in Christ Alan and I went to a meeting in Chandler to investigate a business opportunity. We were taken to this beautiful office building and had to wait for another person to show up before the tour began. While waiting I noticed that the reception desk was adorned with stainless steel covering. I asked the receptionist did she know how amazing this metal is, if you just know how to tap it, things can happen. I showed her my hands and asked if she could see anything in them and when she said no, I snapped my finger twice and produced the Ten Commandment coin.

She said, WOW! I like magic! I told her it was a commemorative coin with the Ten Commandments on one side and the Gospel of Jesus Christ on the other. I mentioned that most people I meet do not know the Commandments but that it would be a good idea if she knew them as one day, she could be judged by them.

Being she mentioned she liked magic, and the person we were waiting for hadn't shown up yet, I stated that if she liked that one then she would love this one. I took out the Red and Blue illusion and she was amazed!

I told her that her eyes could fool her couldn't they, she said, "Yes". I then asked if she would sell one of her eyes for a Million Dollars, she said no! I asked how about both eyes for ten Million, still no. Then I stated that her eyes were precious to her, weren't they? She said yes!

I then said maybe we should look at what Jesus said about our eyes, that if your eye causes you to sin then it would be better if you plucked it out because it would be better to enter Heaven with one eye then to be cast into Hell with both. If that were true then maybe we should look at the other Commandments He gave us. The 9th, had she ever lied? She said, "Yes", What would you be called? She said, "Liar". The 8th, not to steal, she said, "Yes," I then asked what do you call someone who does that, she said, "Thief". The 3rd, was not to use God's name as a curse word, again she said, Yes.

I told her God was very serious about that one! He stated that He would not hold anyone guiltless who did that. He takes it seriously and yet most of us think nothing about doing it, and she agreed. I asked her if God were to judge her based on those commandments and we only did three, would she be innocent or guilty? She said she would be guilty.

I then asked where would God have to send her, Heaven or Hell, she stated, as most of us who have the wrong concept of who God really is, ...she said Heaven. I asked how could that be as she just admitted to breaking three of God's Laws and there were seven more to go. She stated that the Commandments were probably not what God would judge her by, because if He did, then everyone would be in Hell. She then stated how she had been a good person and tries to live a good life by thinking of others.

Next I explained that God has given us His Law and He stated that they are written on our hearts. She knew it was wrong to lie, steal and swear, so if He is a just God, He would have to punish those who do it. I mentioned that time doesn't forgive sin and that one day we are all going to face Him and we will get what we deserve!

I asked again, where would God have to send you, Heaven or Hell? She then changed her demeanor and with her head down stated that she would go to Hell. I asked if that concerned her and she said, "Yes!"

That's when I asked her, did she know what GOD did for us so that we wouldn't have to go to Hell? She said, "He died on the Cross." I then said that's not it, yet many people wrongly believe that. That would mean everyone would be going to Heaven.

I gave her an example that if I had broken man's law and the judge was going to sentence me to jail or if I could pay a fine of $100K, I could be set free. Sadly, I didn't have the $100K. What if suddenly someone came into the courtroom and gave the judge a certified check for it, the judge could let me go, right? She agreed.

I then said that's what Jesus did for sinners, like me and you. He paid the fine for the crimes we committed against a Holy God and because of His shed blood, death and resurrection He saved us from that punishment. What we need to do is REPENT, turn from our sinful lifestyle and place our trust in Him alone!

I suggested when she was at home tonight to seriously consider what she just heard and ask God to reveal the truth about her eternal life, as I didn't have the power to change her heart, only the Holy Spirit can do that. I left her with a few more Tracts and she thanked me for sharing with her.

I then explained to her that those of us who claim Christ as Lord are commanded to do. The Love He poured out for us even though we don't deserve it, is to share with others that we encounter so that they too may have a chance for eternal life.

Her name is Mariah, so pray that the Lord can open her heart and the truth sets her free! Just as we finished up with the tour another high-level person greeted us and thanked us for going through it and stated that if we join them in this business, we would be millionaires! You guessed it! Everyone in the group as well as this executive and the guard got a Million. Again, you should have seen the excitement on their faces!

Thinking the day was done, Alan graciously asked if I would like to have lunch as he knew of a Chinese restaurant nearby. Inside was a little helper who was obviously part of this Chinese family as she was helping clean up the tables as the customers left. I called her over and asked, "what was her name", she said, Joyce, she was nine yrs. old.

I asked how would she like to see what magic this silver teapot had that was on our table. With two snaps of my finger a silver coin appeared! You should have seen her face as she exclaimed WOW, how did you do that. I told her it was a commemorative coin and that it had the Ten Commandments on one side and the Gospel of Jesus Christ on the other and to have her parents read them to her.

This place was small and her excitement caught the attention of the others who were eating as well. Her mom and aunt who worked there asked if I knew of any other magic tricks. I then showed them the Red and Blue illusion card and they were amazed at that as well. They were enamored with the illusion and I told them to read the back as it had an important message on it.

Yep, all those who were working in the restaurant got a Million as well, and even the customers. As we left, we were thankful that the seeds of His Word were placed in the hands of those who may never have had the chance to have them.

What came to me at the end of this day was that I would be sending this out to over 200 of you who could also be able to share using this Biblical principle that is taught by The Way of the Master.

Let's do the math! 20 Tracts times 200 laborers for Christ is 4000 people who in one day would have received the Word of God. I'm sure our Heavenly Father would be well pleased that each of us got out of our comfort zone to do that. Remember what Jesus went through for us at the Garden of Gethsemane? "Not my will but Your will be done! (Mark 14:36)

Driving on Bell Rd, a Driver Signaled Me

In Phoenix Arizona

While waiting for traffic to move on Bell Rd, my eye caught a driver just ahead of me to my right waving his hand out his window saying something.

I rolled down the passenger side and heard him ask me, "Does conflict of interest apply in the business world?" I heard it but didn't understand really what he wanted and then the traffic started to move. I shouted back that if he wanted my answer to pull into the shopping center ahead. I got out of my car and approached his passenger window and again he asked the same question. Puzzled, I asked,

" Why are you asking me that question and why would you care about my answer?"

He told me that he and his girlfriend, who was sitting in the back with a little baby, were arguing about it as she was working for two different companies who did the same work. He was telling her that it was a conflict of interest and she shouldn't be working for both companies.

Again, I asked what made him think that I would be the one to ask? He stated that when he saw me, (you're going to love this) that he thought I looked like a wise man. I was surprised at that answer and then gave him my answer about it.

I replied that I thought that maybe he wanted to speak to me because of my license plate, "IM4GVN", as I saw a fish on the back of his car and wondered, did he put it there? He said no as it was there when he bought it. He then asked what did the letters mean, and I told him it meant:

"I'M FORGIVEN"

He then asked me why. What did I do the I needed to be forgiven? I told him that I used to think that I was a good person. Then I asked if he thought he was a good person, he said yes! I then asked if I could test that by using God's Ten Commandments to see if it's true? He said, "sure go ahead"

He admitted to lying stealing, blasphemy and lust. With each answer his head bowed down as if he was sorry for what he had done. I asked how did he think God would find him, innocent or guilty? He said guilty, I asked where would God have to send him Heaven or Hell? Again, with his head bowing down, quietly he said, "Hell." (Now is the time to ask the most important question.) Does that concern you? He said, "YEA!"

I then asked if he knew what God did for him so that he wouldn't have to go to Hell? He then said that he asks to be forgiven, as he remembers being taught that in Church, and tries not to do them again. At that point I asked him did you not say that the lady in the back is your girlfriend and that the baby is yours? Again, his head bowed down as he softly answered, "yes" and then said that when I mentioned about lust it really made him think about what he had done.

I then explained that asking forgiveness was not enough that he had to have remorse, regret, Godly sorrow for offending a Holy God. It's called *REPENTANCE,* so that you would hate the sin as much as God does and not do it again. The only thing that could save him was to place his faith and trust in Jesus Christ alone. Once he did that, he would receive the Holy Spirit and be *BORN AGAIN.*

At this point now, I'm sure that the Lord had led me to this man as he then asked me, " do I teach others?" I told him yes, as I have a free seminar planned for March 26th. He then said that he would love to come to learn. Please pray for this man, Kim and his girlfriend, as they know have had the opportunity to see themselves as God sees them, not good, (Isa. 64:6)

Though it's not a pleasant experience, it's better to find out now when you still have time to do something about it, rather than to have to face a

Holy God after you've taken your last breath and have no defense because you tried to get in on you own, and that would leave you guilty.

I give thanks to the Lord for sending Ray Comfort to our country and giving him insight on how to teach anyone who claims to be a follower of Jesus Christ how to speak to perfect strangers about their eternal destination. For the first eight years of claiming Christ as my Lord I shared only with my immediate family, a few friends, who after giving my testimony told me they were glad that I found something.

I can't remember ever speaking to anyone else who crossed my path. But in the last six years after taking The Way of the Master Training, I have interacted with over Ten thousand people! I pray that you would want to be a laborer for the Lord as well. (Luke 10:2), (Mark 16:15) (Acts 1:8)

Way of the Master Seminar

July 2010

Today was a glorious day for the Lord as the truth of the Gospel was revealed to several of those who attended the Way of the Master seminar at Kineo Church in Phoenix.

After watching the 2nd video in the series, of Ray Comfort explaining about True and False converts, one lady stood up and calmly stated, "This was the first time in the fifty years she being a Christian that she clearly understood the difference between legalism and a relationship with Jesus Christ. She had admitted that she rarely spoke to people she didn't know but now can see how easy it would be by using the Ice Breakers from this training and she is now anxious to go out to seek and save the lost.

Another man stood up with a surprise in his voice and stated, *"There're wrong!* I have friends of mine from Churches who have told me that The Way of the Master principle of sharing the Gospel is wrong and shouldn't be accepted, but now that I have heard it for myself, I can clearly see that it presents the truth, the Word of God from the Bible, and *They are wrong!* in making that statement!" Another lady stated that she wanted to be refreshed as she had attended one of the seminars about three years ago.

Then Joe told everyone that he had been to a couple in the last 6 months and still wanted to hear more. I guess the phrase,

"Repetition is the mother of learning" has some truth in it"!

After the training about half of those who attended came with us to Tempe. In fact, the agenda is to get as many people out into the streets to watch how easy it is using these principles, God's Ten Commandments, printed on paper that you can offer to anyone who passes you by. (Luke 10:2)

The place we stop at is in front of the Post Office. Other sowers came down as well, as we were able to fill up the corner with these Saints who have a desire to reach the lost no matter what the cost. Al, who also teaches at the seminar, this time brought a 6 foot wooden cross, click to view it on his blog, with him that he made, with the words, "Are you Ready?" written on it.

Alan, Marcus, Joe, Leigh, David, Harry and of course my devoted wife Catherine, who helps me put these seminars on. (I thank God for her!) We gathered together and prayed before turning our attention to those passing by. It was a very quiet night and not many people passing by.

Because the first half hour seemed quiet, Catherine felt the need to pray for more people to accept our offerings of these Gospel Tracts, because the few who were passing by were not taking them. She prayed that the Lord would send us people so we could hand out the Word of God using our Gospel Tracts. Then the Lord was faithful in answering her pray, when several minutes later she noticed that more groups of people were coming by and more Tracts were being accepted.

This was David's first time attending our seminar and coming to Tempe. He was enamored with the magic light fingers that we use to toss back and forth to get the attention of those who are walking by. Several times groups will stop in wonder about us tossing the lights to each other and then we can explain how their eyes can fool them and what Jesus told them they should do if their eye causes them to sin. Now we have their attention and we can politely ask them about the rest of the Commandments that one day God will judge them by and how do they think they would do?

Now, David is thinking about getting these magic light fingers for himself and then he too can look like a fool for Jesus! Wouldn't you have a desire to do the same?

I thought I'd share a strange encounter with one large heavily tattooed man, as I have never been told this before.

I was offering free ice-cold bottles of living water to anyone who could prove he was a Good Person. This man took the challenge and I explained that I would use God's Ten Commandments as the bench mark for his goodness.

After asking him if he ever lied, or stolen he responded with telling me he was Michael the Arch Angel, and that he could kill me right now if he wanted to.

At that moment, I have to tell you that I believed him, because of the look in his eyes and him leaning towards me. I can only attest my calmness through the Holy Spirit as I immediately responded with, "yes you could," but you can only kill my body as my soul is already sealed with Jesus Christ in Heaven! (Mat 10:28)

He backed away mumbled something and I asked if he would like some ice-cold living water? He said okay. I asked if he wanted one for his girlfriend, he said, "Yes!" I gave him another bottle. Please pray for this "Arch Angel", that the demons release Him and like Paul, he finds the truth in the Gospel of Jesus Christ who can save him for eternity. Several hundred Gospel Tracts with God's Ten Commandments were handed out this night, so please pray that by His Grace many will understand why they need a Savior.

I just got this information today and felt compelled to share it with you.

Kevin C. said...

These seminars are really a great way to learn how to share the gospel that God has so graciously given us. My wife and I have attended a few of these seminars and have found them to be powerful times of study and a good fellowship with fellow believers. Tom has spent a lot of time and money to purchase all the resources (the DVDs, books, gospel Tracts, and food [if you go with the group to witness afterward]) and it shows the value he sees in reaching out to lost people and in instructing the Christians that ought to reach the lost also. We have gone out several times with Tom (and on our own) to pass out gospel Tracts, witness to people, and provide instruction to fellow believers; it is true fulfillment of your calling

Thanks, Tom, for conducting these seminars.

Husband and Wife take the Good Person Test

August 2010

Not too many passing by, but the Lord did send this couple to hear His Word and He opened their hearts and minds to the truth...Glory to God for this blessing!

Watch as this couple at first try to justify what they have done and their misunderstanding of a God that was only loving and forgiving. It's sad that they haven't been told that He is also Holy, Just and a Righteous God who must do what He stated: "But for the cowardly and unbelieving and abominable and murderers and immoral persons and sorcerers and idolaters and all liars, their part will be in the lake that burns with fire and brimstone, which is the second death."(Rev 21:8)

But after they heard how the Law would have to punish them for what they had done, they understood what it really meant for them to be Born Again. They would have to place their faith and trust in Jesus' death on the Cross for saving them from spending eternity in Hell and Repent, turn from sin. Just trying to be a "good person", wouldn't save them. If you can hear what the women in the wheelchair said at the end of the conversation," God sent you to us tonight for a reason!"

I post these videos and many photos, Not to show what I do, but to show that any of us can share with anyone about someone who can save anyone, you just need to be willing to learn how to.

Just go to: **www.tillthenetsRFull.org**

AL said...

No one got mad, no one was offended, and they actually thank you and shake your hand when you explain the Truth to them. THAT is the power of
God though Biblical witnessing!

And "Christians" don't want to do this.... why?

Stone Age or New Technology
September 2010

Al, Alan, Marcus, Joe, Ronnie and myself came out to seek those who may be lost.

It's by the Lord's authority and blessing so we know that we have to pray before we encounter them. For our struggle is not against flesh and blood, but against the rulers, against the powers, against the world forces of this darkness, against the spiritual forces of wickedness in the heavenly places. (Eph 6:12)

Shortly after we were prayed up, we started to implement the new tools that the Lord has prepared for us in this time frame. It saddens me to see so many who claim Christ still living in the "Stone Age"! (I'll explain later)

We have these "Rubber Tipped Light Fingers" to draw them away from the bond of Satan for a little while so that they can hear the truth about Jesus Christ. (Would you be willing to be a fool for Jesus?)

These Light Fingers are rubber fingers like those that were used by people who count money, but inside they have a tiny battery and light that when you squeeze it, it lights up. We stand on opposite sides of the sidewalk and throw the imaginary light back and forth to each other. You should see the looks on the faces of those who walk between us. Some will even duck as they pass by so as not to be hit by the flying light.

One such group of about eight well-dressed young ladies stopped in awe, as what they were seeing they couldn't believe. As soon as that happens, one of us will go up to them and show them that this is an illusion and that their eyes could fool them... and as always, they readily agree.

Now is the perfect time, as they are now curious about what they saw, and we can recite a script from the back of this new technology. Ray has designed two curved cards, one Red card and one Blue. When these two cards are held together, they look the same size, but when you separate them and move them from left to right, the Red one looks bigger than the Blue one.

The fact that they believe their eyes can fool them we then ask if they would sell one of their eyes for a Million Dollars. NO, is what you usually get, (unless they are teenagers, then you have to lower the amount because they would sell one for a Million), we then ask how about Ten Million Dollars for both eyes, NO! Again.

Now we give them the reason. We ask them that their eyes are precious to them, aren't they? They always respond with a YES! Now we are free to tell them what Jesus said in (Mark 9:47) "If your eye causes you to stumble, throw it out; it is better for you to enter the kingdom of God with one eye, than, having two eyes, to be cast into Hell." We now tell them if that's true let's look at the other nine Commandments that He gave us.

When they were asked had they ever lied, all eight said yes. When asked if the ever stole anything, several stated that the were Christians. I then asked does that mean they have never taken anything that didn't belong to them? They all said, "NO!" I then stated so if you broke God's Law, would just saying you're a Christian save you from God's Wrath?

With that several grabbed their friends and said they had to go. Our guys gave them all Million-Dollar Gospel Tracts and asked if they would please read them. As they were walking away you could hear them say,

"Thank You for sharing"

Maybe, just maybe using the Law as Paul states in

(Gal. 3:24) we are able to help them understand.

(Check out 1 John 5:20)

One of my favorites from Charles Spurgeon: "I do not believe that any man can preach the gospel who does not preach Law. The Law is the needle, and you cannot draw the silken tread of the gospel through a man's heart until you first send the Law to make way for it."

I hope you can see by using up to date technology we are able to reach those who are lost. This group of young ladies did not have a clear understanding of what it means to be Born Again. If it weren't for the Light Fingers, they never would have stopped to listen to us. If we were to use Stone Age technology and just preach to them, that Jesus loves them, they never would have stopped to listen.

Read (1 Cor. 1:18)

Soon after they left Al and I started throwing the lights around again and this time a family of four stopped to watch. We gave the sane message. I hope you can see that this way of sharing, using these state-of-the-art-equipment, just like we no longer use typewriters, we have computers with word processors.

I'm sure you would agree that if you don't have a person's attention you can't share with them. Ray Comfort from The Way of the Master has several eye-catching items to help you reach the lost. Million Dollar Gospel Tracts, Red and Blue illusion cards. A card that says if you don't think you need a ticket to get to Heaven then tear this up...and they can't. One of my favorites is a shining silver coin with the Ten Commandments on one side and the Gospel of Jesus Christ on the other, just to name a few.

Help me out with this one, give me a good reason why a follower of Christ would resist giving out of these coins, or any of the unique Tracts to everyone you meet? I don't get it! Do you realize how many people we could help find their way to the Cross...talk about a revival! I pray that you would contact me if you're not doing everything possible to reach out to save those who have not received the undeserved gift that you have.

2 comments:

BILL HUNT said...

> WAY OF THE MASTER is great! I've passed out the Million or trillion bills or the ten commandment coins. It's amazing how many divine appointments God arranges just in passing out Tracts. I'm a sower! Come visit my blog site. I'll continue to follow yours.
>
> In Jesus Name,
>
> Bill Corner Retreat
>
> September 28, 2010 at 9:20 AM

AL said...

> How can we not share the Gospel? We are commanded to do so by our Lord and Savior. Jesus said, "Why do you call Me Lord and not do what I say?"
>
> Even atheists understand this. As Penn Jillette (an atheist) once said, "How much do you have to hate someone, believing that eternal life exists, and not tell them that?"

Is it TRUE, you just need to BELIEVE?

September 2010

A young man stopped by to take the Good Person Test, and received his cash for answering the question.

When asked if he was good enough to get into heaven, he said, yes! After taking him through the law he accepted the fact that he was guilty but that he believed in Jesus and was going to Heaven, but did not consider himself a Christian!

He then made an incredible claim, that he also believed in the teaching of Mohammad, and Buddha as the same! I stated that didn't make sense, if you say you believe in Jesus then you should also be called a Christian. Believing in Jesus is an exclusive relationship and if you claim you believe in others for your salvation then you couldn't be saved!

At that point he got very angry and shouted at me saying that if I was telling him that the people who believed in those religions were going to Hell, he then threw the money at my feet and yelled, " I don't want any part of your Jesus!"

(1 John 5:11-13, 1 John 5:20)

Your comments welcomed about this.

On a more positive note, Ronnie is a new sower. This is only his 2nd time out on Saturday night and already he's engaging with strangers! Ronnie was handing out Million Dollar Gospel Tracts on Mill Ave Tempe. Praise the Lord for this man! He now has the courage to share with strangers. He told me that since he had read Ray's book and attended a Way of the Master training, he realized that for all the years he'd been claiming to be a

Christian he had not been obedient follower of Jesus Christ. He now knows that he must be out sharing with as many people he can.

1 comment:

AL said...

>Even the demons believe... and shudder.
>
>Those who think that all religions are the same, obviously haven't even taken a brief overview of the differences.

Friday Night at the Art Fair

September 2010

$\mathcal{A}$nother Glorious night for the Lord! We had some new sower's come out to reach out to the lost.

George and Sarah from Cave Creek came down to reach out and pray for us and the lost. Alan, my loving wife Catherine, Joe, Marcus, Phil and his group was there as well.

Even our atheist friend Sean and his lady friend setup besides us with their large amplifier to try to over shout our ability to share with those who come to listen.

Joe stepped in front of Sean as he was screaming the answers to the trivia questions and started praying for him. Sarah was behind Sean praying as well. Take this at face value because according to Joe, Sean started to stammer and then went quiet.

I try not to pay attention to what that group is doing when I'm trying to draw a crowd, so the only thing I remember was that the shouting from the atheist Sean had stopped. I learned about what Joe and Sarah had done much later in the evening. Praise the Lord for confining those who would oppose the Word of God being proclaimed to the masses in the streets. (1Cor 6:9-10) is very clear!

Reaching out to the lost in Tempe AZ.

September 2010

Saturday night in Tempe was another Glorious evening for the Lord.

During one of our encounters in drawing a crowd with trivia questions a family passed by and the teenage girl answered the question and took her prize of one dollar. I then asked if she would like to take the Good Person Test and she glanced at her father and mother who really didn't say anything, so the young girl came towards me to take the test. Immediately her younger brother came alongside her as well as he too was anxious to get the five dollars that I was offering for the test.

This is the first time that I can remember giving this test to someone so young. I asked her father how old was his daughter, he told me she was 16, so I thought she was old enough to understand what I was about to ask her.

Interestingly enough she had no problem admitting to lying, stealing, swearing, but her brother did. He did not want to admit to stealing until I questioned him further. Letting him know that God was present and for him to search his conscience.

Remember "Con" is with and "Science" is knowledge, so with knowledge, he was convicted about his sin. After that statement he admitted, with a smile on his face, that he had taken things that didn't belong to him.

After admitting that they were law breakers, I asked where would God have to send them, Heaven or Hell? The young lady replied to Hell… and when I asked, did she know what God did for her so she wouldn't have to go to Hell she stated, "He died on the cross".

I then asked does that mean that everyone will be going to Heaven? She said no! So, then I asked did she know what she needed to do so that she would go to Heaven? Her response was typical…just try to be good! I explained what Jesus Himself stated in (Luke 13:3),

" I tell you, no, but unless you repent, you will all likewise perish."

So, trying to be good won't save you. You must place your trust in Jesus Christ alone and then REPENT! (have sorrow, remorse, regret for what you have done that caused Jesus to be crucified.) Then turn from your sins. Ask the Lord to help you HATE the sin the way He HATES sin. This way you won't be a slave to it. No one does to himself what he hates.

Even though she and her brother failed the Good Person Test I gave them the $5 to show a paltry example of what it looks like on how we are saved. I gave her (Ephesians 2:8-10), to remind her it's by grace, not of works that we are adopted into the Kingdom of God.

What happened next, I was not expecting. The two of them returned to where their families when standing and the father came up to me and thanked me for sharing with his children. He then handed me a $5. I told him I couldn't take it as it was freely giving to his son and daughter. He then gave me a big smile and said you don't understand, anyone who preaches the Word of God like that in public deserves it, so that I could give it to some else.

1st Friday Night at the Phoenix Art Fair
October 2010

Tonight, was an awesome night for the Lord! Alan and I went down together, and several seed sowers showed up.

Dana (she likes to be called Dan a' Sounds like banana), David, Joe, Pastor Jon, Leigh, Marcus, Phil, Robert, and Valerie. The Lord definitely was providing support in our endeavor to reach out to the masses on the streets of apathy.

The Lord would have been pleased to see His followers planting seeds to those who may be lost. Would you agree that by going out into the streets where the masses are that it would be honoring our Master? He told us that if we follow Him, He would make us fishers of men. (Mat 4:19, Mark 1:17) We would deny ourselves and take up our cross. (Mat. 16:24) And of course knowing we couldn't do it without His help, He tells us how we will be able to accomplish what He has commanded us to do! (Acts 1:8)

Please correct me if I'm wrong

- Does anyone know of a fisherman who does not go out to fish?
- The fish don't come to them, do they?
- Denying ourselves and taking up our cross doesn't sound like doing the things that we like to do, does it?
- Doing only what's comfortable to us or convenient doesn't sound like the burden the Lord was taking about either, does it?

His prayer in (Luke 10: 2) was for the Lord to send out more laborers, because the laborers are few...

Are you one of the few or the many?

I had one young man tell me that his father told him, that when Jesus came, that He abolished the Law and mankind was no longer under the Law. All that was needed now was for us to Love our neighbors. I asked him had he read that himself in the scripture and he said, "No". I asked if he would like to read what Jesus said in the Bible and he said, "Not really, that I should meet with his father and show him.

How sad it is that the phrase, "I know what I know so don't confuse me with the facts!" Seems to be so popular.

It's starts in (Mat. 5:17), "Do not think that I have come to abolish the Law or the Prophets; I have not come to abolish them but to fulfill them. 18 For truly, I say to you, until in and earth pass away, not an iota, not a dot, will pass from the Law until all is accomplished. 19 Therefore whoever relaxes one of the least of these commandments and teaches others to do the same will be called least in the kingdom of heaven, but whoever does them and teaches them will be called great in the kingdom of heaven.

So, what's your take on this? Does it read that if we are out teaching others about God's Ten Commandments, we are pleasing the Lord, but if not... Well you read the verse and come to your own conclusion.

Wednesday Morning at McDonalds
October 2010

After this morning's breakfast the Spirit of the Lord compelled me to write what happened.

I pray that when and if you read this you understand I'm not trying to make a statement, "Look at Me!" But with just a small amount of Biblical training, look how the Lord can use even me.

This story would not have happened if I was not prepared to share with a perfect stranger. I truly believe the Lord wanted me there!

- I was supposed to be someplace else
- I was about to leave,
- I sat in a place where I would not normally sit.

Here's a question!
Strangers cross our paths all the time, so how do you approach them?

This morning I went McDonald's around 11:00 for a breakfast burrito. I was told by the young man behind the register that it was too late as they now had their lunch menu up. I struggled to order a burger and he kept asking what would I like to order. No one was behind me so I just kept staring at the menu trying to decide what else I could have. I then noticed a woman beside me so I told the young man to serve her.

After a few minutes another young man behind a register asked if he could help me. I went to him and stated that I wanted to have and egg burrito but was told it was too late, and that I was going to leave to find another place to have breakfast. He stated that they had some left and if I wanted one, he could get me one. That made my morning! Praise the Lord!

A few minutes later a Postman came and sat near me and I noticed that he put his head down before he ate his food. I thought to myself was he praying or just thinking about his day. I took one of the Million Dollar Gospel Tracts I always carry and said, "Excuse me but were you just praying before you ate?' He stated, "Absolutely!" I then said to him, "Well whenever I see someone praying to the Lord, I give them a the Million

Dollar Gospel Tract".

He gave me a big smile, as that's what usually happens and then said that he had one of these and he had it stuck on his wall. At that point I asked if he had read the back and he said yes and he remembers seeing these given away on TV. The guys who were doing it were

Ray Comfort and Kirk Cameron.

That's when I said to him well how did you get that first Million, and he said, "Someone gave it to him." Then I reminded him that's what he needed to do. Written on them is the Word of God and they are meant to be shared with others so that they too can read why Jesus Christ died for their sins.

He looked at me with a strange look at first then said, "You know your right." I asked him had he shared the gift of salvation with others that cross his path and he admitted sheepishly, "no." But he said after watching the program, it convinced him that he should be reaching out to others, as he has never heard a message like that from anyone else.

I then mentioned that I was putting on a seminar to teach those who claim to be followers of Jesus Christ, on the last Saturday in Oct. I asked if he would like to attend? He stated that he wanted to learn more but said he couldn't come because he works on Saturday.

I then said that I would teach him one on one whenever he had the time, as I could hear from our conversation that he wanted to apply what he had seen from watching The Way of The Master on TV. He then said what if he had some other men willing to attended, could they attend as well?

Praise the Lord again for creating an opportunity to raise more laborers! (Luke 10:2)

Posted by Thomas Fusco at 10:33 AM

4 comments:

Anonymous said... Make it so Tom, make it so.
God bless, Joel, B.

Anonymous said...
Praise the Lord!

> I guess this should be encouraging to me. We are to arrive in AZ next week. Our church is doing a Rick Warren small group event in IL. I was disappointed because I would have liked to attend, but we are leaving here on Sunday. Then, I got the brain storm to do a small group in AZ, in unison w/our church here. Yikes, I definitely do not think that I am qualified, and am now thinking I shouldn't have gotten involved. If I don't chicken out, I hope Our Lord uses me for the good in spite of my fears.
> Please pray for us in this endeavor.
> Love, Barbara, C.

Saturday Night with Tree of Life Church
October 2010

Saturday night was another glorious night for the Lord!

Pastor B. J. and his people from Tree of Life Community Church in Tempe just finished their training from the Way of the Master on Thursday night and were now out on the streets of Tempe to put into practice what they had learned from the three previous classes.

It's truly amazing to watch those who come out as they are at first hesitant to speak with the strangers who pass by. But I reminded them that I was the same way in the beginning when I first attended a Boot Camp in Seattle WA.

When I was there, it took a couple of hours for me to rely on the Holy Spirit, to energize me, and to not think of what they may think of me when I approach them, but to think of their faith, as this might be the only time anyone confronts them about where God might have to send them on Judgment Day. A fiery existence for eternity!

Do nothing from selfishness or empty conceit, but with humility of mind regard one another more important than yourselves; (Philippians 2:3)

And so, it began. We all teamed up and prayed as we encountered the crowd by first offering Million Dollar Gospel Tracts to those who were passing by.

Later Al and I did some Open Air, where we offered money for trivia questions to try to draw a crowd, so that more could hear what God has in store for those who deny Jesus as Lord and Savior. (John 3:18)

Later on, I asked if they would like to try to hand some out? Some said they would try, others sheepishly said yes. It was exciting to watch these new sowers reach out to the lost with their new weapon, Million Dollar

Gospel Tracts with a few of God's Ten Commandments on them. Now they would experience for themselves as to how easy it was to say to a passing stranger, "Did you get one of these?"

You should have seen how excited they were when the first person who walked by took one…the Joy it brought to them was exciting to watch to say the least, as now they were answering Jesus' prayer in Luke 10:2.

Later that evening I asked Pastor B J what he thought, now that he had seen how we use these Gospel Tracts with the some of the Ten Commandments, and Open Air to draw a crowd, so we can ask those who stop by if they would like to take "The Good Person Test".

He responded with an excited response! He would like to have his people get more training so that more of his people would learn how simple it is to reach out to the lost. And also, that his prayer that he has been praying since January would be answered,

"That, the Church walls would come down!"

The Phoenix Magazine Knows about us!
It's not a Secret ANYMORE! October 2010

The other day a blessed sister in Christ, Jean a passionate Seed Sower for the Lord, (or you could say Evangelist) called with excitement in her voice, as she stated, "You made it!

They have you in the magazine!" Catherine and I met with her as she showed us the magazine,

"Phoenix Magazine which posted 101 FUN Things to Do!"

CAN YOU BELIEVE IT?

Here's what it says. Evangelical street-preachers. Atheist street-preachers. Crypto-hippie homeless dog owners. Steroid-popping bar backs. Press-on-nail center maidens. We could go on all day. Without a doubt, Mill Avenue in downtown Tempe boasts the most diverse human ecosystem in the Valley. After you turn 30, it becomes harder to justify actually going into any of the bars, but Mill's people-watching pleasures are an all-ages treat. millavenue.com

Now those who report what is going on using this 160-page magazine think that we are something to come to watch. How exciting is that!

I PRAY THAT OUR CHURCHES WOULD ENDORSE US IN THE SAME MANNER!

I pray that many will come to hear as we boldly proclaim the reason why our Lord had to leave His Heavenly Throne and descend to Earth. His coming was not so that we would just know about Him, or accept Him as we have been told, but that He needed to show us how imperfect we are. (Even the demons believe in Jesus and they shudder!)

He came to show us the standard God requires from us, "Perfection". In (Mat. 5:48) He stated that we needed to be perfect as your Heavenly Father is perfect. How could any of us claim to have achieved such a high standard? What is the standard that we would be compared to? Sadly, most of us compare our goodness to others. It's easy for us to look at others and claim that we are not as bad as they are. Obviously, we have been deceived into thinking that we are GOOD... even good enough to get into Heaven.

In (Mat 5:17) Jesus clearly explained what it would take to be accepted, or as Paul states adopted into the Kingdom.

"Do not think that I came to abolish the Law or the Prophets; I did not come to abolish but to fulfill." He lived a perfect life, just like he proclaimed in (Mat. 5:48). And again in (Mat 19:17) And He said to him, "Why are you asking Me about what is good? There is only One who is good; but if you wish to enter into life, keep the commandments." In (Luke 18:18-20) He explained what we would have to do to measure up to His standard.

Several times in the four Gospels, Jesus states that we needed to keep the Commandments. In (John 14:15) Jesus puts it simply,

"If you love Me, you will keep My commandments."

Now with that in mind, how many of the Ten Commandments can you name? Oh, and for some of you just concentrate on the Ten that God took the time to write on the stone tables. You can find them in (Exodus 20: 3-17).

Remember this is the standard that God will

- Judge you by. Let's try a few to see how you do.
- Have you ever lied,
- Taken anything that doesn't belong to you, (the value doesn't matter)
- Used God's Name in vain, you know swearing. How many of you know that the Lord stated the He would not hold him guiltless who takes His name in vain? (Exodus 20:7) Just that one sounds pretty serious but how many of us have violated that one and many times?

I Pray that you understand the meaning of what I'm saying. This is NOT legalism as some have accused us of. It's just stating the fact, that none of us is good enough to be adopted into the Kingdom. Jesus is very specific as He stated in (Matthew 4:17) and several other places. From that time Jesus began to preach and say, "Repent, for the kingdom of heaven is at hand."

Please help me with this one! It sounds like we have to admit that we are Law breakers and not qualified to be admitted into the Heavenly place with our Holy, Perfect and Righteous Lord. We deserve to be punished, correct? Once that part is clear, I think He has opened our eyes to see how filthy we really are. It's the Grace of God who provides that reality. (Ephesians

2:8-10), reveals that to me. Now because of that knowledge I must REPENT, have sorrow, regret, remorse, not to just turn from my sins but as Jesus told the woman caught in the act of adultery, "Go and sin no more"

Once I realize that I have offended God, and what Jesus had to go through to save a wretched sinner like me, how could I continue to violate the same Laws that Jesus paid the fine for that set me free by taking the punishment that I deserved.

Now that I know why I have been set free and have been adopted into the Kingdom of Heaven. I MUST, I MUST, be an obedient servant and do as my Lord and Savior commands...

Go and tell everyone I meet!

Our Seed Sower Team in Tempe Saturday

November 2010

This night, Al, Anne, Dan, Jean, Jennifer, Joe, Leigh, Luke, Marcus and myself trying to keep warm on a cold November night.

This cold night didn't stop those who had a desire to reach out to the lost. It was a Glorious night for the Lord as we had several one-on-ones, and did some Open Air's.

One of the team members got over her fear of speaking to a crowd and stood up on the step stool and with microphone in her hand to proclaim what God had given to Moses on Mt Sinai. She quoted in order the Ten Commandments, the measure that God has given mankind of what He expects from those who claim Him to be Lord.

Don't take this out of context, I not saying keeping them is what will save us, as we know that it's by Grace we are saved. (Ephesians 2: 8-10), tells us that. But how many even know them? I've asked hundreds of people who claim they do, but when I asked then to name them usually can name only three or four.

It seems like our team of sowers is growing. Praise the Lord that more laborers are coming forth to proclaim what it means to be adopted into the Kingdom of Heaven!

Sharing Jesus Christ on ASU Campus

November 2010

Today a bunch of us we went to ASU to share the Gospel of Jesus Christ with those who may be lost.

Below are some of the team members.

Al, Ann, Jean, Jennifer, Jill and the others came out because they have recognized that just being a pew sitter is not what it means to a follower of Jesus Christ. Jesus' prayer for those who claim him as lord is that our Heavenly Father send out more laborers because the laborers are few! (Luke 10:2)

"Are you a Good Person?"

There were many other sower's as we had 2,000 Gospel Tracts to hand out and the fish were definitely biting. Besides handing them out, many of the students were curious about what the message was and many of us we were able to do what is called "One-on-Ones"!

Pray that our Heavenly Father desires to adopt these sheep who are lost, as they seem to follow the campus philosophy that God isn't real and we are fanatics. What should concern us is that if we just keep quiet, as this is what our culture has endeared to us to do, you know "whatever", we shouldn't be telling others what the truth is as long as they believe in something, they are okay!

But what did Jesus tell us in (Matthew 10 :34)? We need to be stirring up the pot because when people are complaisant, they are not motivated to do anything. Have you heard how you can boil a frog to death? When they are in the pot of water very slowly turn up the heat.

It seems we are the same, as long as I'm comfortable living my life my way I'm fine. What would it take for you to be on Fire for the Lord, and boldly proclaim what a wonderful, gracious, everlasting gift you have received? Maybe reading what Paul himself wrote and prayed for in: (Ephesians 6:18-20)

One other comment, by sharing what the truth in the scriptures reveals to others we are called judgmental and that's not acceptable behavior. But can you help me with that one, because if someone claims that I'm being judgmental, then, aren't they being judgmental?

This young man didn't get offended or stated that I was judging him by asking him if he considered himself Good enough to get into Heaven. After asking him how would he be found if he had to face God after he admitted to lying, stealing and having lust in his heart, he admitted he would have to be sent to Hell. This concerned him and after I explained what Jesus had done for him and that he needed to REPENT and place his trust in Jesus Christ ALONE, for the forgiveness of his sins, he thanked me...WOW!!! praise the Lord for this divine intervention.

1st Friday Night with a man on his knees

November 2010

It was an inspiring evening to say the least! To watch Al's eight-year-old daughter McKayla, not just recite the Ten Commandments but she nailed them perfectly!

I was also inspired to see all those who showed up: Al brought his wife Jill and their daughter McKayla, Ann who came all the way from Avondale, Alan, Toya and Dana, who brought Susan (this was her first time), Marcus and his sister Jennifer, and of course my lovely wife Catherine. It was also a blessing to see and hear those who stand on the rock in front of the Scientology building who proclaim the Gospel of Jesus Christ.

I was also blessed to see my good friend Dave the laborer for the Lord, who has recently returned from his outreach in Japan. It looked to me as if we are beginning to answer the Lord's prayer instead of us always asking Him to answer ours. "Send more laborers" (Luke 10:2)

This night was truly a blessing from the Lord as He answered our prayers by bringing many crowds to me so they could take the Good Person Test. One man after taking the Good Person Test, realized that he had failed miserably, and was headed for Hell! To my surprise he immediately got on his knees and I asked if I would pray for him. I told him that he should pray to the Lord 1st, and then I would pray for him.

I don't know about you but to have someone go down on his knees before me and ask that I pray that his sins be forgiven is something, I'll never forget!

Truly, Truly, the Lord was giving me a BLESSING!

Catherine's Mom Burial January 2011

I would like to share with you what happened today.

*C*atherine's mom died December 26, 2010 the day after Christmas and then in January her family had the internment. That's where they place the urn with the ashes in the crypt on the church grounds.

As I walked to the place where they were going to place the urn. I notice there was a carving in stone of a book on the ground that looked open that was about four feet wide and three feet high. The words I saw really caught my attention. On the top of this carving, which looked like a page were the words The Ten Commandments. On either side of this carving were engraved all of Ten Commandments. I couldn't believe my eyes and wondered what message the Episcopalian Minister was going to give to the family.

Before we went outside to the site, he showed a good sense of humor as he was telling of us how many times that he hiked the Grand Canyon. I didn't have a relationship with him as I'd never meet him before so I thought I would comment on his wit and good sense of humor he possessed. I then asked him did he know how priests make holy water. He laughed and stated you just take out all the lies out it.

I then told him what I heard was that you just boil the Hell out of it and he laughed and agreed. That's when I asked him then why do priests go through the motion with their hands and say there are blessing the water? He shrugged that one off by saying, "well that's just the way we do it." As we got closer to the entrance there was a stone sculpture of the book of Exodus 20 verses 3-17, God's Ten Commandments.

I then asked him why did they have this part of the Bible here? He said he didn't know. I then asked him if he knew what the 9th commandment stated; "they were all in his head." Then I asked again, could he recite it for me because I have found that very few people can. He now stated he wasn't sure so I told him what the 9th Commandment was, and asked him if he had ever lied? He was quiet and responded, "that it was all about how wonderful and loving God is."

A Cold Saturday Night in Tempe On Mill Ave.

January 2011

Tonight Al, Catherine, Joe, Marcus, Ronnie, and were some of the faithful sowers who came out on this cold winter night in Tempe on Mill Ave, to reach out to the lost.

I purchased some Glow Sticks which lite up when you bend them and they glow with different colors. The light at night attracts some who are walking past us at the Post Office where we hang a sign, "Are you a Good Person?" We explain to those who stop that we are giving away Glow Sticks to anyone who takes this test.

Lyquidia and Marsherrie, were one of the first to stop by after I mentioned that we were giving away these Glow-Sticks to anyone who would take the Good Person test. Lyquidia responded quickly. I told her that I was going to use God's Ten Commandments to see if she was, not my opinion or the world's point of view.

She agreed and then I asked if she had ever told a lie as the ninth Commandment God said that we were not to lie. She smiled and stated that everyone lies, I agreed but then reminded her that this test was about her and not the other people in the World.

She then said "yes", and so it went as I asked her three more, which she admitted to breaking. The 8th, stealing, 3rd Blasphemy, and finally the 7th, where Jesus explained that even if we lust after another person, we have committed Adultery with that person in our hearts.

At this point she became a little more agitated and stated that she didn't like where this was going and now was not liking me very much. I then asked her if she had ever heard the phrase, "Don't shoot the messenger, but listen to the message!" It was a real blessing for her as her friend Marsherrie spoke up and said, "yes", as she had heard her Pastor explain it.

Marsherrie then made an extremely encouraging comment. She told her friend that she should listen to what I was saying and be thankful that it was being explained to her." Praise the Lord for Him bringing these two ladies to us and pray for Lyquidia to have the Lord help her recognize what her sins are and repent from them, and place her trust in Jesus Christ alone for the forgiveness of them.

Just as they were leaving Marsherrie said to me, "This was the most extremely important message she had ever heard and she thanked God for bringing me out onto the street tonight to speak it to them!"

I gave another test to two young men, Tabby and Alexander, who are in their early 20's, who both after admitting being guilty of violating God's Law proclaimed, they would be declared Innocent because God is a loving and forgiving God, and wouldn't send anyone to Hell.

I then gave him a courthouse scenario, how a good judge must punish a law breaker. I also explained to him what it meant to "REPENT "to have remorse, regret, to be sorrow for offending a Holy God. The young man Tabby then proclaimed that he knew all about Jesus and His death on the cross, but was not willing to turn from his life style as he liked it the way it was. He then made an amazing comment. He might repent of his sins when he was in his 40's.

I then asked him how long did he think it would be before he would die? He pondered for quite a while and then stated around 70 or 80. I then asked had he heard about the shooting deaths in Tucson where several people were killed, one a little girl age 9? He said he had. I told him that he really couldn't tell me how long he might live as he could die tomorrow and then where would he wind up as he just admitted he wanted to keep on sinning for at least two more decades.

His demeanor changed after that comment. I could see in his face the realization about what could happen was now real. I asked him if he would read some other information that I had and when he went home tonight that he gets on his knees and ask the Lord to show him how he could redeem himself. By his desire to please Satan and continuing to live in sin, does not please the Lord. By having a changed heart that would be pleasing to Jesus. Now what is needed is to truly repent of your sins and place your trust in Jesus Christ alone, and that will save you from eternal punishment in Hell.

We continued on for most of the night, as I was able to interact with several people that night because of the silly Glow-Sticks. Please consider learning this simple Biblical principle, God's Ten Commandments, on how to reach out to those strangers who pass you by every day. They are possibly being misled and need to hear the truth!

A Night to Glorify the Lord Jesus The Christ

January 2011

Tonight, was an amazing night. I got an email who was a friend of ours' telling me about their son Addison who is 18-months old, now in the hospital.

Catherine and I went to visit and found that the boy was improving... Praise God! We were able to share with several of the hospital staff including the volunteer person who escorted us to the room, as we gave her a Million Dollar Gospel Tract for taking us and explained that she needed to read the back to find out if she was Good enough to get into Heaven.

As we were leaving, I asked a man which way to go to get to the exit. He was kind enough to give us a long explanation of all the turns we needed to make. With that I gave him a Million for being so helpful and then he stated that he would take us to where we needed to go. While walking I asked him who was he here for and he told me about his 5yr. old daughter who was in for over a month and had brain surgery removing a tumor.

Now at the door I showed him that a silver coin can appear from the chrome handles of a wheelchair, and gave it to him explaining that it was a commemorative coin and that it had the Ten Commandments on one side and the Gospel of Jesus Christ on the other. Then an amazing thing happened...he asked if I would come back with him to show what I just done to his daughter.

I looked at Catherine and we both said yes. When we got to the room the little girl was sleeping and several of the family members were there. Think of the opportunity presenting itself, as now I was able to offer everyone a Million Dollar Gospel Tract. The man's wife then asked if we could come back about an hour later as they would have to wake up their daughter up to get her ready so she could sleep for the night. With that request, how could we refuse! We left to get something to eat, and came back about an hour later.

The little girl was now awake but I could see she was sedated. She did give us a slight hand wave to acknowledge our presence. I showed her the coin trick and placed it in her hand as she could barely raise her hand. The father and mother were very appreciative that we came back, so that's when I showed them the Red and Blue illusion cards again, in more detail. The wife was enamored on how her eyes where fooling her and then I walked her through the Law and the consequences of violating them. I summed up that all the religions in world were a false representation of trying to get to Heaven.

Some religions pray to a priest to have them forgive them of their sins as I was once Catholic and that's what I was taught by them. But now my eyes have been opened and I know the truth. Now I mentioned to them the only way that I can be accepted into the Heavenly Kingdom was that I needed to repent of my sins, lying, stealing, cursing, and lust to name a few, and place my trust in Jesus Christ alone to forgive me.

A nurse came in and we were going to leave, but that's when I was convicted that we needed to pray over this little girl and I asked her parents if it would be okay and asked them to come close to their daughter and we all laid hands on her and Catherine and I prayed.

Now comes the amazing part that Catherine and I got a kick out of. I hope you continue and don't stop reading yet. The father asked me what my name was as he really appreciated us being there. Now here it comes. You're going to love this...really, he said his name was Moses....Moses! So now I can say, I finally met Moses!

A Banner Asking,
ARE YOU A GOOD PERSON?

February 2011

*H*ere is our new banner that helps to draw those who think that they "*Are A Good Person*"

I hang the banner in front of the Post Office on Mill and 5th St in Tempe. Even in the rain many stopped by to get their free souvenir a, Large Colorful Glow-Sticks.

Using this concept groups of people would stop by and claim that they were GOOD and what test would they have to take to receive their free souvenir?

This presented a great opportunity to ask them if it where okay to use God's standard to see if they qualify as being GOOD! Each one of these groups said no problem. It truly is amazing how many who claim to be brought up in church when they admit to be a lawbreaker state that their God would not punish them for violating God's Law. Here are some of the more popular responses:

1. They said a prayer when they younger
2. They try not to sin anymore
3. Jesus is a loving God and wouldn't send anyone to Hell
4. They do a lot of good things, like attend church, give to the poor

They are stunned to learn that the God they have been told to worship, is the same God that Paul talks about. (1Co 6:9-10) Or do you not know that the unrighteous will not inherit the kingdom of God? Do not be deceived; neither fornicators, nor idolaters, nor adulterers, nor effeminate, nor homosexuals, nor thieves, nor the covetous, nor drunkards, nor revilers, nor swindlers, will inherit the kingdom of God. God is Holy, Just and Righteous and must punish the wicked otherwise

He would not be a True God.

The only acceptable answer for the forgiveness from God is for them to Repent, (have remorse, regret and a Godly sorrow for violating a Just and Holy God), then place their Faith and Trust in the only one who can save them, and that is Jesus the Christ.

When that happens, the Holy Spirit indwells in each one of us whom He has called to be adopted into the Kingdom, and as Jesus stated:

"Come follow Me and I will make you fishers of men!"

Fishermen don't sit in the cabin next to the lake they get out of their seats and go where the fish are.

Now, if you're having a problem fishing please give me a call, and prayerfully with the help of the Holy Spirit we can help.

I Will Make You Fishers Of Men

1st Friday Night at 3rd and Roosevelt Phoenix

February 2011

*F*riday night was freezing cold, yet some of us braved the low temperatures and showed up at 3rd and Roosevelt to reach out to the lost.

It was mentioned to me that no one would be out because of the cold, but how would we know for sure unless someone went out there. Alan, Ron, and I got there around eight, and a little while later Mike D. showed up and a little later Steve T. showed up from the church, I used to go to.

It was exciting to see these two new men from different churches, get out of their comfort zone to learn how to reach out to strangers. Steve stated that he wanted to come to my next seminar, and is committing to coming out with us a least two times a month. Again, the streets were flowing with hundreds of people. Praise the Lord for giving us the desire to conquer our doubts about the freezing weather.

I did a few open airs and was saddened to hear how the youth of today, those who stopped by to take the good person test, seem to have no conscience! When asked if they ever lied or stolen, they respond with laughter and pride, and when asked what do people call someone who does those things, they said, "**human**".

One stated that it would be okay to kill someone who was a very bad person. When I asked what standard would he use to validate that, he stated, "none", he would just know who was very bad. As cold as it was, the five of us we're able to hand out hundreds of Tracts.

Thankfully I was able to give one young man a Bible. After I was finished sharing God's Ten Commandments with one of his friends he came forward and asked some great questions about what I had just said. I asked if he had a Bible at home, he said no, so I asked would he read it if I gave him one, he said, "yes".

Praise the Lord with God's blessing, the next 1st Friday we will be there. My pray is that some of you can join us so that you can have the blessing we get by knowing we are being obedient and faithful servants of our Lord and Savior Jesus Christ!

Saturday Night with Catherine
March 2011

Catherine and I arrived later than normal on Mill Ave in Tempe, as we were invited to a ST Patrick's dinner and didn't get there until 9PM. I must confess, we found it difficult to head down to Mill after the dinner as we came home to change our clothes.

I go often and I had to force myself this time NOT to stay home and just relax after an enjoyable dinner. We could have found lots of reasons not to go. Prayerfully when we arrived, Al, Alan, Marcus and Ronnie were already there passing out Tracts.

Catherine had taken a large handful of the Million Dollar Gospel Tracts, about 200, before we left for the dinner and commented that she would like to leave around 10-10:30PM, as she had a lot to do Sunday and wanted to get up early to get them done. She stated that she probably grabbed too many Tracts as she couldn't see how she would be able to give them all away in just an hour.

Time certainly fly's when you're having fun and just past 10 Catherine mentioned to me that she only had a few Tracts left and couldn't believe how many people passed by her accepting the free gift. Once they take it Catherine always prays that they read later and that the Lord would open their hearts. She was extremely excited as she now realized that just being obedient, as she really didn't want to go to Mill Ave so late and to leave early, and yet the Lord blessed her and lifted her spirits as to how successful she was just because she came out to the street.

One young man stopped to asked her about what she was doing handing them out and she told him it was a Gospel Tract and if he read the back it was worth more than a Million. He read some of it and then stated he knew Jesus and sometimes went to church. He also spoke of how when he messes up, he asks for forgiveness and knows that God is loving and forgives him.

I then asked him how often does he ask to be forgiven? He stated several times a day. I then mentioned that I didn't hear him saying anything about repentance, since Jesus stated in (Luke 13:3), that unless you repent you all likewise perish. Paul makes a similar claim in (2nd Corinthians. 7:10), For the sorrow that is according to the will of God produces a repentance without regret, leading to salvation, but the sorrow of the world produces death.

At this point he started to explain how he really wasn't willing to give it his ALL, as he liked doing what he was doing and when that day came that he would be willing to give up his life style, he would accept all that Jesus required of him, but not yet.

I tried to explain to him that maybe the Lord brought him to us tonight and this is the time for him to humble himself and to repent of his sins, have remorse, regret for offending a Holy God and not do them anymore. To consider asking God to have him hate the sin as much as God does, because you never know when you going to take your last breath.

I asked if he remembered the student who was killed here on campus a while back, he said yes, but just then a young lady came up to him who obviously was intimate with him, snuggled up to him and said let's go. He left with a smile and said, see how hard it is?

A few minutes a group of four came by and took a Tract from me and when they realized we were sharing Christ they stated that they were Christians, and didn't need one. One had two large black circular rings embedded in his ears with several nose rings as well. I don't understand why the youth of today think they have to defile their bodies. After a few of his comments about how loving God is and He wouldn't send anyone to Hell.

I then asked if he considered himself to be a good person, and would he mind using God's Commandments to validate it. As usual he said yes, and then I asked the other guy and the two ladies to take the test as well. The two ladies answered quickly about lying, but the man with the earrings refused to answered and only replied with that he was saved by the Blood of Jesus.

After a while he commented that I sounded like those people who believe that I was chosen by God and NOT of my own free will, and he didn't want to talk to anyone like me because we were spreading lies. The God he believes in, which he himself sought out at age seven, is a loving God and would not send anyone to Hell. The lady next to him then stated that the questions I was asking was not what Jesus would do and that I needed to show more love.

When I asked her had she ever read the Bible verse from (Luke 18:18) where Jesus Himself used the Commandments, she said yes, but the way to share with others is to do it as she does. She explained how she sat on a bench with a homeless person and just asked about his life. She could see how amazed he was that she would sit with him. She told him how she was sexually abused growing up as a child and had a lot of anger and bitterness in her.

When she accepted Jesus, also at age seven, she forgave her molester and became a Christian. After her sharing her experience with this homeless man she made an amazing claim, that he accepted Jesus and became a Christian.

I then asked if I could summarize back what I heard her say? It sounds like if I have had a horrible experience in my life, been molested, no money, relationship breakups, then all I need to do is accept Jesus, because He loves me and I will be saved.

I then asked her what would I be saved from, as it appears that God has burdened me with unimaginable situations when I have done nothing wrong. Then those of us who have not been molested, have adequate finances and a well-rounded relationship don't need to accept Jesus? That's when she said it was a waste of time talking to me and they left.

Comments about this Biblical Principle from my Blog

Sarah, George said...Hi,

I love the repentance explained part so much. I praise our Dad for drawing that couple to the mystery of the cross, the resurrected living Jesus, so that the Godhead will indwell in them. And I will pray that the H S will continue to point Jesus to Him the way, the truth and eternal life and live in Him.

Thanks Sarah, George March 17, 2011 at 1:52 PM

Anonymous said...This is really a Wow!
Wise, he was right about that, but thinking that of you driving, it was God's plan for them Tom! Love u! March 17, 2011 at 1:53 PM

Christy said...thanks for sharing another encouraging story! I will pray for this young couple and their baby.
God is abundant to provide what we often see as "chance encounters" it truly takes so little effort on our part. -- just to be ready when it happens. God can even make us "look" wise :-) - that was awesome! Hee hee! Have a great day!
Christy March 17, 2011 at 1:53 PM

Good job Tom. Obedience is better than sacrifice. Jeff

My name is Liz
I'm a member of Ray and Kirk's ministry team. They have entrusted me to answer some of the e-mails that come into the ministry. I Thank you very much for your encouraging words; you have no idea how much they mean to us. We are so glad that you are blessed by this ministry. I have a friend

from this ministry who loves to personally tell people all the time that there has never been a ministry before or since that has blessed her like this ministry has, and I can't agree more. I am excited that you too are encouraged by this ministry.

Thanks again for taking the time to write! March 18, 2011 at 3:38 PM

My Name is Valerie Wow!

What an amazing day you had out in traffic, Tom! That experience had to be arranged by the Holy Spirit. It was one in a million...maybe a billion! To God be all the Glory! And thank you for sharing it with me! I am making a copy of your account right now, so I can practice saying a few of the statements you made to the gentleman.

Thanking God for you and Catherine! Valerie March 19, 2011

Jeremy and Tish wrote:

"Praise God! Our Lord is so mighty and so amazingly awesome! Thanks for sharing this encounter with all of us Tom!! God bless you :)

Tish" March 19, 2011 at 8:55 PM

Saturday Night in Tempe then Taco Bell
April 2011

This night was similar to the other nights. Asking everyone if they would like a free Glow-Stick.

To get one all they have to do is prove they are good enough to get into Heaven. It amazes me how many stopped by to get them, even the men want them. It's in ([Proverbs 20:6](#)).

"Most men will proclaim everyone his own goodness: but a faithful man who can find?" (KJV)

Al did an open air and the man who came forward to take the good person test walked away when he realized he was guilty before a Holy God. When Al tried to help him understand what he needed to do to be right with God he walked away and gave Al the finger gesture, which is common to those have nothing to say.

You must give credit to Al for taking a risk by speaking to a perfect stranger on how to avoid the pitfalls of Hell. Obviously, this man and many others who have their own view of what God is like needs our prayers.

We left our corner around 11PM to get a late-night snack at a Jack in the Box. Marcus and Kat came by to meet us. We started talking about our Baptism experiences and I shared how one day the Lord provided me the opportunity to Baptize four people in one family and three of our friends on the same day.

There were three young men seated near us and one of them asked if they could ask a question about Baptism. He asked, " is it necessary to Baptize babies?" I asked, "What do you think?" This started about an hour-long discussion about Catholicism verses Christianity.

Now, many questions were asked about Catholicism. Marcus, and his wife Katrina, along with Al addressed these points about the falseness of this religion. Below is what they insisted is their beliefs.

- Babies must be Baptized to cleanse them of original sin
- We must speak to Mary for our prayer request as she was born free from sin, (God would not place Himself into a sinner's body)
- When the Eucharist is offered by a priest, it has become the actual body of Jesus, because the priest has that power to transform it
- Holy water was next, again the priest has the power to bless it and make it holy, (I then explained that the only way to make water holy is to boil the Hell out of it... as nothing on Earth is holy only God is Holy)
- We must confess our sins to a priest as he has the power through God to forgive us our sins so that we can get into Heaven (Last Rights?)

These three men were adamant about what they believed. What made this divine appointment amazing to me was their response to the question I asked,

" What is your religious background?"

The first man stated that his parents were from Saudi Arabia and he was raised Catholic. The 2nd one was raised Catholic as well with American parents, but the most unexpected answer I got was from the man who stated that he was raised as a Muslim, and just recently converted to being a Catholic.

Can you believe their last statement about confessing to a priest for forgiveness? I asked them a hypothetical question?

If they were told that they were dying, but maybe a doctor could save them, and having only one choice, a doctor or a priest, which one would they choose? Immediately, without hesitation they stated,

"A PRIEST!"

With that answer I explained that they have a false religion. They are being taught to place their faith and trust in a priest instead of the only One who can save them from the pit of Hell, Jesus Christ. (John 14:6) I told them that my answer, as one who has been born again, would be a doctor.

I'm so thankful that the Lord placed these men in my path. I'm also grateful that I was out that night like many other Saturday nights seeking to save the lost. Not only was our message heard by them but as we were leaving Al mentioned to me, "Did I see all the other people in the restaurant standing behind listening to what was being said?" I had not, as I was focused on speaking to the men in front of me. He marveled at how many were standing there drawn to listen about God's Word.

I myself was raised Catholic and was taught to do all the same religious acts that they professed and tried to please God and to also place my faith in priests.

Please pray for others like this as the Scripture is very clear,
 (Matthew 7:15, Matthew 24:11, and Matthew 24:24)to name a few.

Comments from Way of The Master Seminar

May 2011

The first one is from a 15yr old boy.

I really liked the seminar you guys had.

I was really interested how Ray Comfort and Kirk Cameron went out on the streets and told people about the LORD JESUS CHRIST. It was so cool I can't wait until I can go on Saturday to Tempe. And also, with the bag of The Way of the Master ice breakers, I showed some of my friends what they were and what they are meant for and they liked it as well. Thanks for showing us the videos. See you later.

Sincerely,

Forest

Hi Tom, thanks for the reply. Man, it was a great day and the impact of it is still sinking into my being. I had some things I had to attend to after the meeting but Lord willing, I would like to go out and join you the next time. I did the good person test on my wife and she was stumped and so I am excited about the whole thing, kind of like being born again for the second time only better cause we have gained in wisdom over the years.

I enrolled in the WOTM School of Evangelism today and spent the afternoon watching past shows of On the Box. The one thing that you mentioned about denying the Lord and having Him deny us before the Father in Heaven resonated with me because there have been so many missed opportunities over the years that are gone due to my own flesh or pride or whatever it was, I simply did not speak up when I should have. I feel like maybe this is the chance to turn my life around and do the work of losing my life for Christ and finding it, rather than saving my life and then losing it later. I hope to get to know you and the others on the team more and just be faithful to the call that is placed upon us. Let me know when you plan on going out okay? Take care,

Dave.

Hello Tom and Catherine,

I was extremely tired on Saturday due to only sleeping about two hours the night before. (A combination of work and teenage son drama...) That being said, I came away with a newfound hope that even I, a nobody, can positively impact somebody's life for Christ. I have great respect for anyone who witnesses the Good News of the Gospel on a daily basis. Thank you for your time and efforts.

In His Service,
Joe "Deacon"

Let Your Light Shine

I'm sure you have heard this expression, well Friday night at 3rd and Roosevelt Art Fair was the epitome of that expression!

Even an 8-year-old named McKayla was able to bring a spark to those she went up to. Twice she stood up on a step stool and through a loud speaker boldly quoted the precious Ten Commands to the crowd.

What came to mind was what Jesus tells us in (Matthew 18:3) and said, "Yes! I tell you that unless you change and become like little children, you won't even enter the Kingdom of Heaven!

AL, her father told me later that she had given away hundreds of the Million Dollar Gospel Tracts, during the two hours out on the street which asks, "Are you Good enough to get into Heaven?" So, I guess by what I have been told by those in Church leadership, she has the GIFT of Evangelism. Or maybe she is just being an obedient child who places her trust in her loving father to do what he has shown her to do.

If Jesus is the Lord whom you claim, commands you to go out and share, (John 14:15, John 15:14, Mark 16:15, Acts 1:8), to name a few, would you not be counted as one of His children if you did?

What come to mind is Mathew 7:21-23, "Not everyone who says to Me, 'Lord, Lord,' will enter the kingdom of heaven, but he who does the will of My Father who is in heaven will enter. "Many will say to Me on that day, 'Lord, Lord, did we not prophesy in Your name, and in Your name cast out demons, and in Your name perform many miracles?

"And then I will declare to them, 'I never knew you; DEPART FROM ME, YOU WHO PRACTICE LAWLESSNESS.'

Now we had a stream of people who walk by us on Friday night parading to get a free Glow-Stick, if they take the "Good Person Test".

Listen to the excuses of those who attend church on how God is only a loving God and would not punish those who continually violate His commands. Hebrews tells us differently! (Hebrews 10:26-29)

Our culture has been trained to create a God that suits themselves, one that agrees with what they believe, and their god would not send anyone to Hell. There right their god couldn't, because he is just a figment of their imagination, but the true God the Righteous God and the Just God must punish the Law breakers. (1st Corinthians 1:6-9)

You're going to LOVE this!

July 2011

*T*oday was another one of those days orchestrated by the Lord. I had two appointments this morning that were no shows before 11AM. I tried calling some of my friends to see if they would like to meet. Answer machine on one, answering machine on another. One had just woken up, wasn't feeling well and needed to be resting, better not to come over. (wise decision)

This day happened to be my older sister, Mary's birthday. I thought I'd give her a call even though I thought she would be out having lunch with her children. Much to my surprise she said she was sitting watching TV, so I asked if we could meet for coffee? I told her I was near PV Mall and asked where could we meet and she stated McDonald's.

I tell you this so that can see how the Lord orchestrated this whole morning, as this was not planned by me. About a half hour in our conversation a young boy about five yrs. old came up to our table and asked what were we doing? (I later found out he was autistic) With that my sister stated she was celebrating her birthday with her brother. This cute young boy then said, "that's nice!"

I was so taken by the boldness of this five-year old, who asked a perfect stranger a question. That's when I showed him how the Ten Commandment coin appears out of thin air. I have used this illusion for the last six yrs. This gets people's attention in a way that they want the coin which has the Ten Commandments on one side and the Gospel of Jesus Christ on the other.

After his excitement about seeing it appear, to my amazement three other children a few years older approached me and asked if I could do it again with them.

This part is awesome, just as I finished giving each a coin, then four more children came by and wanted it done to them. I now had about six or seven children alongside our table all excited. I then notice that my sister was hysterically laughing, and states that she had never seen so many excited children at her table.

Yes, and the adults that were their got the Million Dollar Gospel Tract. They all thanked me and went back to their separate tables. Well this part should grab your heart, one of the adult ladies came back after a while and stated that she was the young boy's guardian who came to our table 1st, and that he was autistic, and that I had just made his day!

Talk about being "BLESSED!" If I didn't learn how to make a coin appear out of thin air, how would I have been able to bring such joy to those strange children. The one that touched me was the five-year old who had autism.

Remember what Jesus said,

"Truly I say to you, unless you are converted and become like children, you will not enter the kingdom of heaven."
(Matthew 18:3)

I can only thank the Lord and the Holy Spirit for providing me with the desire to reach out to anyone about someone who can save everyone, even if it means I might make a fool of myself.

1st Friday at Phoenix Art Fair

August 2011

What can I say that I haven't said before! This Friday night was like any other 1st Friday night where the lost come in droves to stroll up and down Roosevelt Ave in Phoenix, AZ. This gathering seems to be different than when we go out on Saturday nights to Mill Ave in Tempe. They are not walking alone. They come with a friend or several friends. Many are there with their whole families, they even bring their babies in strollers.

Too many times I have been told from the Christian community that they cannot come there because they are spending time with their children. Why not come and spend some time with your family, so by example, teach them how to reach the lost?

As I set up the sign that asks if they would like to have a souvenir, if they can prove that they are a "Good Person", those who are curious start to hang around. Maybe these are what I have heard some churches state that are, "Seekers"! But those of us who know scripture, that's not true. They are either lost or saved! When I bring out the Glow-Sticks, and ask who would like one, these few seekers become a mob.

This night was another blessing for the Lord! He used these Glow-Sticks like the miracles He performed 2000 years ago. I'm not saying this is just like the miracles He performed, I'm saying the drawing of the crowd is what it must have been like when those who saw the miracles told others and that's when it became a large crowd.

When I was finished taking the first group of about 20-25 people through the test, another crowd was waiting to answer the same questions. I started about 8:30PM, and didn't stop till around 11PM. I gave the same Gospel message about why they need a Savior. What is so sad is that of the hundreds of times that I have asked the question, "would God find you innocent or guilty to those who admitted breaking just four of His Commandments, the majority answer "INNOCENT!"

When, I ask how can that be, they tell me that God is loving and forgiving. This is the most popular answer from those who admit not attending a church as well as those who claim to be Christians. Last night was the worst abomination I have ever seen!

I had in front of me about 30 young men and women who claimed that the Lord loves homosexuals. They were constantly trying to explain their lifestyle. Not only were they screaming that at me but one young girl stated that she was attending seminary and was taught that the Bible stated that the Lord loves homosexuals. I hope you can handle this part... two of the men came up next to me and starting kissing each other for about five minutes in a very passionate way.

Should we be quiet about what the Lord says about homosexuality?

(1Cor. 6: 9-10) "Or do you not know that the unrighteous will not inherit the kingdom of God? Do not be deceived; neither fornicators, nor idolaters, nor adulterers, nor effeminate, nor homosexuals, nor thieves, nor *the* covetous, nor drunkards, nor revilers, nor swindlers, will inherit the kingdom of God."

Shouldn't we be bringing the truth to the streets?

Can you see the possibility, that we could reach more of those who are held captive by Satan where they are hanging out, then by trying to bring one or two of them to the church?

Here we have The Lord Himself, making this statement in (Mark 16:15),

"Go into all the world and preach the gospel to all creation."

Then in (Acts 1:8), here He telling us why we need to have the Holy Spirt to help us be His obedient witnesses!

"but you will receive power when the Holy Spirit has come upon you; and you shall be My witnesses both in Jerusalem, (Phoenix) and in all Judea (Tempe) and Samaria, (Scottsdale) and even to the remotest part of the earth."

He commands us to **GO,** to reach out to the lost! How about **YOU GO** out, and then answer His prayer. (Luke 10:2)

"The harvest is plentiful, but the laborers are few; therefore, beseech the Lord of the harvest to send out laborers into His harvest."

Experience the joy of knowing that you are being an obedient servant for the Lord. (John 14: 15).

"If you love Me, you will keep My commandments."

Saturday Night on Mill in Tempe Arizona

August 2011

𝒫raise the Lord as tonight was exciting as we had laborers for the Lord from both sides of the valley. Each participant had to travel about thirty-minutes to get there. Ken, being his first time coming to the seminar, came from Avondale. Brandt and his wife Haley, who live in Queen Creek. Jeremy and his wife Tish, brought their son Joshua came from Mesa. Marcus and his wife Katrina brought their son Alex from Maricopa.

Catherine and I set up the sign asking, "Are you a Good Person, take the test and get a free souvenir" Lately, instead of offering money to answer trivia questions to draw a crowd, I now offer to give away free Glow-Sticks. I don't get it, what is it about a Glow-Stick that draws so many groups of people to take the test to get one.

Shortly after announcing that I was giving them away to anyone who can prove that they are a good person, I had four young teenagers, three guys, and one girl, stopped and raised their hands. I asked them if they considered themselves to be a good, which they all said yes. I then asked them that I would be asking them some questions to see if it were true. I was not going to use my opinion or the world's point of view, but God's Ten Commandment, would that be okay?

I say this to you so that you understand that I don't trick anyone into answering them, I make it very clear how we are going to come to that conclusion.

After they admitted to breaking four of the most common, I asked how did they think God would find them, innocent or guilty? They all responded, "innocent!" I then asked how could a Holy, Righteous and Just

God find them innocent when anyone who breaks God's Law would have to be guilty? They then said they were leaders from Young Life and their God was a loving and forgiving God.

I tried to explain that God was not only a loving God, but a Righteous, Just and Holy God and because of that He must find a Law breaker guilty, or He wouldn't be God. I also mentioned that I hadn't heard anything from them about repentance, Godly sorrow, that Jesus spoke about. Again, they defended their position that Paul said that they only needed to believe in Jesus and they were saved.

I then asked, saved from what? They already admitted to lying, stealing Blasphemy and lust of their heart, and it doesn't seem like you have any remorse. So, if they have been given this information by the church they attend, that your God is a loving and forgiving God, then based on that statement alone, every human being is going to Heaven and no one would be going to Hell. We need to be careful about what we say to those who are lost and not give them a false God to worship.

Jeremy spoke to them that if you only speak of God's love and not the Wrath of God then you have created a God that is not the God of the Bible.

I find it sad today as so many who are being raised in the church have been told of a false God, that Jesus, or God is a loving God and now believe that their sins are forgiven.

One problem, Jesus Himself states in several places, from that time Jesus began to preach and to say, "Repent, for the kingdom of heaven is at hand." (Matthew 4:17, Matthew 11:20, Mark 6:12, Luke 13:3,5) where Jesus repeats Himself, TWICE.

Peter, in (Acts 2:38, Acts 17:30), states, "Truly, these times of ignorance God overlooked, but now commands all men everywhere to REPENT. "

Revelation mentions REPENT several times as well.

(Revelations 3:3) is one of them.

So where am I wrong?

Tell me if you have been told the same message as these youngsters. Maybe it's time we speak the whole truth to those who are in and out of church!

Spenser Taking the Good Person Test
September 2011

Spencer tries to partly defend his position of knowing how to be forgiven and yet hasn't done it.

This man is a stranger who lived in Flagstaff to get his degree from NAU. He now lives here in Phoenix. I asked him that according to what Jesus stated about the Samaritan, isn't this man someone that we all should strive to engage the whole truth with.

In Luke 10:29-37, But wishing to justify himself, he said to Jesus, "And who is my neighbor?" Jesus replied and said, "A man was going down from Jerusalem to Jericho, and fell among robbers, and they stripped him and beat him, and went away leaving him half dead." And by chance a priest was going down on that road, and when he saw him, he passed by on the other side. "Likewise, a Levite also, when he came to the place and saw him, passed by on the other side.

But a Samaritan, who was on a journey, came upon him; and when he saw him, he felt compassion, and came to him and bandaged up his wounds, pouring oil and wine on them; and he put him on his own beast, and brought him to an inn and took care of him."

On the next day he took out two denarii and gave them to the innkeeper and said, 'Take care of him; and whatever more you spend, when I return, I will repay you.' "Which of these three do you think proved to be a neighbor to the man who fell into the robbers' hands?" And he said, "The one who showed mercy toward him." Then Jesus said to him, "Go and do the same."

Notice this was a "priest" who crossed the street, a Levite also crossed the street. What name would you give those people today? Is it you? Jesus showed them who a true neighbor was. The one who goes out of his/her way to interact with someone in need.

But it's not just about bodily care or financial assistance, it's about saving souls! Notice what Jesus said in Matthew 18:11. **For the Son of man is come to save that which was lost.**

Now I ask?

- Do you avoid those who cross your path?
- Do you avoid strangers?
- Do you only speak to family, friends, and co-workers?

If you answer yes, then are you not like the parable above?
Charles Spurgeon said, "If you have no desire to save the lost then you are not saved yourself… you can be sure of that."

If you would humble yourself and admit this is a problem for you, I pray that you attend one of the Way of Master Seminars…it could help you become a laborer for the Lord, instead of being just a pew sitter.
Catherine has made this comment since she has attended the seminar several times which she never could have before:

"I'm a nobody who can share with everybody about somebody who can save anybody" Would you like to be a nobody?

Prayer Alone???
September 2011

If prayer alone is what the Lord wants from those He has adopted into the Kingdom, then why should we go out on the streets like Jesus did to warm them of the impending danger of Hell?

This Saturday night I handed a track to a young lady who immediately stated that she didn't need one because she was a Christian. I then asked her, "why not take it and give it to someone she knows"? She commented, as most who claim to be one, that she doesn't have to because she just prays for them???

Read what Charles Spurgeon had to say about it.

"If you ask God to convert souls, but you will not do anything for those souls; if you ask God to save your children, but you will not talk to them about their salvation; if you ask God to save your neighbors, and you do not distribute Tracts among them, nor do anything else for them, are you not truly a hypocrite? You pray, but you refuse to do anything to affect an answer."- Charles Spurgeon

So, is Spurgeon correct?
Prayer without action is hypocritical? (James 2:14)

What does scripture say? (Ezekiel 3:18-20) "When I say to the wicked, 'You will surely die,' and you do not warn him or speak out to warn the wicked from his wicked way that he may live, that wicked man shall die in his iniquity, but his blood I will require at your hand.

If, however, you are fulfilling the royal law according to the Scripture, "YOU SHALL LOVE YOUR NEIGHBOR AS YOURSELF," you are doing well. But if you show partiality, ("Speak only to your friends and family," my comment) you are committing sin and are convicted by the law as transgressors.

"Yet if you have warned the wicked and he does not turn from his wickedness or from his wicked way, he shall die in his iniquity; but you have delivered yourself. "Again, when a righteous man turns away from his righteousness and commits iniquity, and I place an obstacle before him, he will die; since you have not warned him, he shall die in his sin, and his righteous deeds which he has done shall not be remembered; but his blood I will require at your hand.

For whoever keeps the whole law and yet stumbles in one point, he has become guilty of all. For He who said, "DO NOT COMMIT ADULTERY," also said, "DO NOT COMMIT MURDER." (James 2: 8-26)

Now if you do not commit adultery, but do commit murder, you have become a transgressor of the law. So, speak and so act as those who are to be judged by the law of liberty. For judgment will be merciless to one who has shown no mercy; mercy triumphs over judgment.

What use is it, my brethren, if someone says he has faith but he has no works? Can that faith save him? If a brother or sister is without clothing and in need of daily food, and one of you says to them, "Go in peace, be warmed and be filled," and yet you do not give them what is necessary for their body, what use is that? Even so faith, if it has no works, is dead, being by itself.

But someone may well say, "You have faith and I have works; show me your faith without the works, and I will show you my faith by my works." You believe that God is one. You do well; the demons also believe, and shudder. But are you willing to recognize, you foolish fellow, that faith without works is useless? Was not Abraham our father justified by works when he offered up Isaac his son on the altar?

You see that faith was working with his works, and as a result of the works, faith was perfected; and the Scripture was fulfilled which says, "AND ABRAHAM BELIEVED GOD, AND IT WAS RECKONED TO HIM AS RIGHTEOUSNESS," and he was called the friend of God.

You see that a man is justified by works and not by faith alone. In the same way, was not Rahab the harlot also justified by works when she received the messengers and sent them out by another way? For just as the body without the spirit is dead, so also faith without works is dead.

(1st John 3:8) the one who practices sin is of the devil; for the devil has sinned from the beginning. The Son of God appeared for this purpose, to destroy the works of the devil.

(Jeremiah 42:20) For you have only deceived yourselves; for it is you who sent me to the LORD your God, saying, "Pray for us to the LORD our God; and whatever the LORD our God says, tell us so, and we will do it."

(notice it didn't say just to pray)

Those who were convicted 2000 yrs. ago did not have the written Word as we do today. Our Lord and Master Jesus the Christ's message has been written down for all who claim Him Lord. So, we know what He expects and commands from us.

(Psalm 19:7), says the Law is perfect to use
(Mark 16:15), to GO out tell everyone
(Acts 1:8), He tells us to be His witness

(Acts 10:42), commands us to solemnly to testify

(Galatians 3:24), by sharing the Law we can bring the lost to Christ by Faith.

1st Friday at the Art Fair

September 2011

*A*nother glorious night for the Lord, as His prayer in (Luke 10:2), was being answered.

Again, the streets were overflowing with lost souls just like the hurricane on the East coast produced rivers that overflowed its banks. Tonight, we had many followers who wanted to get out of their comfort zone, and be true laborers for the Lord and not do the typical, just sit home and watch TV.

There was Alan, Alex, Brandt, Catherine, David, Jeremy, Joe, Joshua, Karen, Kat, Marcus, Steve, and Tish, all who came out to honor the Lord's command. Here are a few: (John 14:15, Mark 16:15, Acts 1:8). Oh, and if you would like to be Jesus' friend as I have heard a song sung in church, then you need to obey (John 15:14).

This night Catherine and I brought our 11-month-old granddaughter Addisyn with us. She was such a joy, even the loud speaker didn't prevent her from comfortably going to sleep.

We continued even though it was passed her bedtime.

Jeremy, Tish and their 16-yr. son, Joshua, who just got his driver's license, (please pray for him)! This is the perfect example of the Lord's blessing of a Christ following family.

It's always a joy seeing them together reaching out to those souls who are less fortunate. Jeremy and his family need our prayers as he is now going to start his own church.

Karen, from North Mountain Church, had attended The Way of the Master seminar that I gave at her church in July and this was her first time out. She told Catherine that she couldn't get over how the people who were taking the Good Person Test stayed and listened intently to the end. They did not seem to be offended even after they admitted to lying, stealing, lust in public. Yet, she really couldn't understand why those in church do!!!

Of all the years she has been in church she has NEVER seen anything like it taught. This was the first time she saw this kind of interaction with strangers, and admitted she didn't think she could do it. That's when I asked her if she could sew? She said, "Yes". Then I asked was she able to sew perfectly the first time? She, smiled and said, "NO". That's when I explained that I couldn't do what she sees me doing now either... it took practice and desire.

Katrina brought her friend Laura from CA. This was Laura's first time experiencing how we use the Ten Commandments to help the lost understand why they need a savior. She too was enamored about how those who we interacted with responded to our questions.

Brandt with microphone in hand, stepped up on the step stool to reach out to the tide of people and asked if anyone would like a Glow-Stick. All they needed to do was to admit that they were a "Good Person" and answer a few questions using God's Ten Commandments to see if it were true. You really have to be here to see how many raise their hands with excitement claiming that they are GOOD.

One of my prayers is that the Holy Spirit would work on the hearts of those who claim Christ as Lord and act as His obedient servant by coming out just to watch how many souls can be reached in just one night. I was told that those of us who go out into the night to reach the lost witness to more people on one night than most churches do in a year. (Can you imagine how many people we are reaching in a year?)

After a while because of the crowds in front of us, Alan went across the street as he saw the banks overflowing there as well. He came back about an hour later extremely excited and announced that he had just given away 700 Gospel Tracts with the Ten Commandments on them. He also had several one 2 one conversations asking them if they had kept the commandments and if not, what would a Just God have to do to them. Several seemed to be convicted and pray that the Lord can open their hearts to let the seed that Alan planted take root.

While Brandt was sharing with a group, I saw a young lady off to the side staring at him. I asked if she would like to have a Glow-Stick, she replied, "Yes". I then stated that in order to get one she would have to prove that she was a good person using God's Ten Commandments as the standard. Without hesitation she stated she was a good person and was willing to prove it by taking the test

Well I won't bore you with what happened next a you know she admitted to lying, stealing, Blasphemy, and lust of the heart. She now realized she wasn't good and she would be sent to Hell if she died then. I asked if she knew what God did for her so that she wouldn't have to go to Hell, and she said, "NO". I asked if she had any religious upbringing, she said some, she was raised Catholic.

I then told her the GOOD NEWS, that only through the shed blood of Jesus Christ our sins are forgiven. No Priest can save her. Just because she confesses her sins to a him...he didn't die for her sins, Jesus did!

Then as Jesus states in (Luke 13:3-5), we must REPENT, which means to have Godly sorrow, heart-felt remorse, for having caused His Son, Jesus, to be sent as a sacrifice to pay the penalty that I deserved and now she knows she deserves.

She would need to ask God to help her hate the sin as much as He does. I then told her she didn't deserve the Glow-Stick, as she didn't prove she was a Good Person. Now I noticed that her head hung down and I then stated:

For by grace you have been saved through faith; and that not of yourselves, it is the gift of God; not as a result of works, so that When no one may boast. (Ephesians 2:8-9)

I then told her that this Glow-Stick is a paltry example of what Jesus did for her on the cross and all she had to do was to reach up and accept the free gift.

She reached up, and then thanked me!

I pray that these stories open your heart to want to go and do something different with your life.

Paul states in (Romans 10:17),
So, faith comes from hearing, and hearing by the word of Christ.

When you're out and about, try speaking to strangers.

180 Movie Project at ASU
October 2011

*T*oday was the day that Ray Comfort from the Way of The Master chose to have those who are laborers for the Lord go on the attack and confront 300 thousand college students across the USA, by offering them the free video on YouTube buy clicking the name 180movie.com. Which shows a comparison of the Holocaust in Nazi Germany and the Holocaust of abortion in the USA.

On the College Campus of Arizona State University, 20 of us showed up to do our part by coming together to Glorify God by actively **confronting** the students, faculty, and janitors who passed us by. With all of us spread all over the campus, we were able to give away about 3000 of these DVDs.

In Webster's Dictionary version 1828, one of the definitions for **confrontation** is: "The act of bringing two persons into the presence of each other for examination and discovery of truth."

In today's culture with worrying about not offending anyone, I wonder how many of you would apply that definition in your life?

One of our sowers David told us how a security guard told him that someone complained that they felt that the way it was being offered was too pushy. By this time, we had been there for about two hours so, they probably knew what the DVD contained and wanted to find a way to stop us from handing them out.

The guard then told him that several of them were being stacked up on tables in the cafeteria. He was nice enough to ask David if he would like to have them ad that he would get them for him.

When he came out of the cafeteria, with a pile of them in his hands. I noticed David was busy sharing with someone else, so I went over to him to thank him for being so kind, going out of his way to help us.

I then asked if he would like one but he refused. I then said to him, how would he know about what they were complaining about if he himself hadn't seen what was on the DVD? Wouldn't it be wise for him to know? With that he responded, "good point," took one and said, " thank you."

Now comes the part that only the Lord could have ordained! All 20 of us gathered at the large fountain to see if all the DVDs had been given away.

This section has a restaurant, music and tables that the students put up to display whatever they want. I noticed a very young group of kids about 20 of them, probably from 10-13 years old, all wearing the same colored shirts, and a few middle-aged guys wearing the same. I walked up to one man and asked if I could show his kids an illusion? That's when I showed them that I could make a coin appear from thin air.

I told them not to believe it as it's a trick, an illusion and they should examine what they see, as their eyes could fool them. I told them it was a commemorative coin, with the Ten Commandments on one side and the Gospel of Jesus Christ on the other. With that statement they all shouted," can I have it! " This is not unusual, because 99% of the time I get a similar reaction. Think about it, another way of reaching the lost! Contact me and I'll teach you how to do it.

I gave it to the one who I thought was the most excited, as most of them raised their hands as well. I then asked if they knew the Commandments? Now there was silence.

That's when I asked for help from my team to come and record this, as I knew the Lord had brought me here to boldly speak about His Righteousness and Grace, and it would be through these children that I would have the platform at this campus to do just that!

THOMAS FUSCO

Friday Night at Phoenix Art Fair
October 2011

5. I Pray that you read this to the end.
6. I pray that you ask the Lord on High to keep us humble
7. I pray that He continues to encourage us to GO speak to strangers who may be lost on the streets.
8. I pray that what the Holy Spirit has done in us that you ask Him to do to you as well

Wow, what can I say about Friday night!!!

The Lord has shown us a place, just like in (Luke 10:2), where the harvest is plentiful but the laborers are few.

But praise God and the Holy Spirit, that last night His prayers are being answered. Again, this was an awesome night for the Lord as 100's of Gospel Tracts were handed out. Alan, Erwin, Mike, Philip, Steve, and Brandt and his wife Haley, and another couple Jeremy and Tish and their son Joshua, and another couple Marcus and Katrina and Alex. How pleased the Lord must be to see all of His chosen in the family going out to reach the lost.

Here are a few of us who went out to eat afterwards to relax and fellowship, at 2AM.

These sowers all showed up with one thought in mind, to intentionally confront those who passed by so that they may have the opportunity to witness to those who may be lost. By offering them these Million Dollar Gospel Tracts that ask are they "Good Enough to Get into Heaven", they are being proactive. Remember Jesus didn't wait for others to come to Him, He went out into the streets to reach them…shouldn't we be doing the same if we claim to be a follower? By using His Ten Commandments we can be assured that it's the Word of God being professed and not a man centered watered down comment that God is love and Jesus wants them to have a wonderful plan for their life!

Charles Spurgeon stated:

"I do not believe that any man can preach the gospel who does not preach Law. The Law is the needle, and you cannot draw the silken thread of the gospel through a man's heart until you first send the Law to make way for it."

He was called the Prince of Preachers, maybe we should heed what he says?

Paul states in (Romans 10:17) So faith comes from hearing, and hearing by the word of Christ.

I pray that some of you, this includes those in leadership as well, give up just two hours one Friday night a month to come out and see what the Lord is doing on the streets. Or how about make a commitment just for every other month, you know like when you commit to attending a Bible study. Is that too much to ask to do for the One who sacrificed His life so that you could have eternal life?

He commanded us to GO and share! (Mark 16:15, in Acts 1: 8, Acts 10:42) to be His witness. He died not so that we would have a better life, but He died a horrible death to pay the fine for the crimes that you and I and others committed, like lying, stealing, blaspheming, lust to name a few.

His resurrection from the dead three days later proved He was God and He warned us that we need to REPENT or PERISH. (Luke 13:3-5)

He performed miracles that drew a crowd to hear His message, we give away these Glow-Sticks, it draws a crowd and that crowd gets a chance to hear the truth. The Glow-Sticks are a big hit! It is a non-stop request to get one. I can't explain why they desire them but you'll have to come and see for yourself. You should hear what those on the street say to us when we ask them if they are Good.

It's sad when you hear someone profess to be a Christian and then get offended because you explain what the Bible says about Law breakers. Or to have some Gay people tell you that God is Love and as long as you love, then God is pleased, even if that love is with the same sex partner.

One would have to ask why would someone who professes to being a liar, thief, and an adulterer at heart be offended that a Holy God must punish that person. Didn't the Bible say that Jesus came for the sick and not the righteous? So why get offended? That would be making the statement that you one of the righteous wouldn't it?

So, I'll end with another prayer request, the one Jesus ask for us to do for Him, (Luke 10:2)

"The harvest truly is great, but the laborers are few; therefore, pray the Lord of the harvest to send out laborers into His harvest."

Saturday Night on Mill Ave Tempe
November 2011

*W*OW! Tonight, we had in one place more of those who are concerned about saving the lost then we have had for a while.

It must have been a blessing to the Lord as we all gathered in a circle and prayed that our message would go forth to the lost, of this town and beyond.

Those who showed up were, Edwin, Anna and their baby in a stroller, Rob Roy and Tammie, Phil and Jessica, Tim, Katlyn, Sean and Mia, Cole, Leigh, Alan, Al, Marcus and Alex. After praying we split up to cover several corners so that we could be more effective reaching out to the crowds.

By offering the free Glow-Sticks it still seems to be effective, as I was able to do several Open-Airs to those who stopped by to receive one.

One that comes to mind was three young sisters. I asked how old the one was and she said 16. All three professed to being, a «Good Person». I noticed that they were with a mature couple but the couple continued walking to the corner as the children came back to where I was. As I asked the questions that Jesus used to the rich young ruler in Luke 18:18, a few of God's Ten Commandants.

We need to be careful not to share with the lost a man centered message that makes people feel good about themselves. instead we need to use the Words that Jesus Himself used to help others understand what being GOOD is.

After asking a few of the questions, I turned my attention to that corner and shouted out, "are you their father?" He nodded yes, and that's when I stated that he should be here with his daughters, as it wasn't right for them to be talking to a perfect stranger without him watching over them. He just stood there turning his head from side to side.

Well now the three of them admitted to lying, stealing, and taking God' name in vain. I asked how would God find them, innocent or guilty, because of that behavior, and they stated; guilty. Then came the tough question; "Where would God have to send them if that were true?" Now their chins fell into their chests and without a word they pointed towards the ground. I can't tell you many times that has happened, as those who have heard about Hell have a very difficult time saying it.

At that point I noticed their Dad right next to them. I know he could hear me from where he was standing, as the sound from the microphone I use is loud. This is when he tried to protect them, as he grabbed the arm of one, and said let's go.

That's when I stated that this is what he and his daughters need to hear and they should not leave. (Can you believe it, they stayed!) I now asked the important question; "Does that concern them that they may be headed for Hell? "

I was grateful that they said, "YES" as now I knew that they understood. That's when I shared with them what Jesus did for them, as well as for the rest of us who can't pass the Good Person test.

Once we understand and admit that we rightly deserve Hell and that Jesus' death on the cross is the only payment acceptable to God for our sins. He took the punishment for our sins by shedding His blood, dying a horrible death on that cross, then three days later He rose defeating death. Now if we REPENT, turn from our sins, having a Godly sorrow, remorse, regret, then place our faith and trust in Jesus Christ alone. (Luke 3:3) Our dirty slate will have been wiped clean, remembered no more. It's not what we do but what He has already done for us.

IT'S FINISHED!

(John 19:30)

I give thanks to the Lord on High who allowed that message to be heard by that family who was just passing by and stopped to get a Glow-Stick, as well as to all those who may have heard it on the corner of 5th and Mill Ave in Tempe AZ.

Please Pray for Amanda
November 2011

𝒫lease pray for a young lady, Amanda, as she believes that Mahatma Gandhi is in Heaven. I met her Sat. night on Mill where she was handing out flyers to help encourage those on Mill to go to a certain bar. When she approached me, she stated, "Oh you're doing the same thing that I am! " I said I don't think so as I'm handing out Gospel Tracts so that everyone, I meet will know why they need a Savior.

You do realize that those who had out these flyer's get a fee if someone shows up at the bar with their flyer's. I wonder how many Christians knowing they would be compensated for handing out the Word of God to perfect strangers would be anxious to do so without fear)

This one is about "Which Religion is Right? " She then thanked me for doing that as she too believed in God. But when she looked at Tract and she saw all the different religions she proclaimed that they were ALL right. I asked how can that be when they all proposed a different way. They all required that you work or earn your way to Heaven.

Only one states you are saved by Grace. That's when she got a little agitated with me stated how could I believe that, when God is love and wants everyone to go to Heaven. That's when I asked her if she thought that the people who flew the planes into the World Trade Center are in Heaven? She didn't think so. That's when she brought up Mahatma Gandhi, stated, "Look at all the good things he did, you can't tell me he's not in Heaven!

That's when I asked her if being good was the criteria, would she qualify? She said YES! That's when I asked her if she would mind answering a few questions using God Ten Commandments to see if that were true? She agreed and when I asked if she ever lied, she said yes, I asked what do they call people who lie.... here it comes, she said HUMAN! It wasn't a surprise to me as I get this a lot, most people don't know what SIN is. I explained that she had violated the 9th Commandment. I asked if she had ever stolen anything, again she said YES, and called herself a thief. I asked had she ever cursed in anger by using God's name, again she agreed.

I asked, would a Holy God allow any law breaker into Heaven? She did not respond. I then explained to her the only way is if we admit that we deserve the just punishment for what we did, repent of them, and place our faith and trust in Jesus Christ alone. His death and resurrection paid the fine that satisfied the Wrath of God that I rightly deserved. That's when I shared with her what Jesus stated "I am the way the Life and no one comes to the Father except through me!"

That's when she got angry and walked away.

Please pray for her and all those like her who have been deceived into thinking that God is only love and because of that He wouldn't send anyone to Hell.

BTW, here's a quote from Mahatma Gandhi acknowledged the inability of his religion to atone for sin. Despite his moral lifestyle and good works, he admitted,

"It is a constant torture to me that I am still so far from Him whom I know to be my very life and being.
I know it is my own wretchedness and wickedness that keeps me from Him."

All works-based religions lead to futility and death. It is only in Jesus Christ that sinners can find forgiveness for their sins and deliverance from death and hell.

A Comment from November 2011

In the past you, and I see myself doing this also, preaching at so to speak instead of more so interacting, listening and responding to, with truth in love to those we are witnessing too. One of the greatest dangers in preaching the Law is putting forth a message that we have to be good enough-religion, even if we don't intend to, instead of the truth that we can do nothing apart from Christ.

I think in the video below, your encounter-interaction with the kids, you did an excellent yet simplistic job of communicating that biblical reality. You had their attention; they were engaged by you and It looked as though they actually pondered and comprehended what you were trying to translate to them! You held them accountable and interacting with you by getting them to communicate their responses by raising their hands, etc. And of course, using the Million Dollar Gospel Tracts, etc. as fishing lures so to speak.

So, much today we talk at people instead of with them. And the kids and adults know when someone really cares. I know this to be true; They don't care what you know till they know how much you care. So, may we be the most caring and proficient communicators for God's glory and a great harvest Amen. One of the main evidences of fruit is the feedback.

I've learned to ask, what did you hear me say? You will learn about them and yourself this way. You solicited such responses in the video with hands, expressions and their words. Maybe you're learning to listen and discern more now by the Spirit, I see that in fact actually.

Though when you're in His will Tom it is just natural and thinking about it too much only messes you up so just keep praying studying the Word and being obedient to His calling and He will use you and me, etc.!!!

We sow and water and the Lord, He gives the increase!!!

Praise God!!! God Bless!!!

Signed, Bo.

Jacob Takes off his Rosary Beards

December 2011

Saturday night was quiet, as I think most of the students went home to be with family. It seemed like the parents of the students were out with them as most of those who passed by were in groups of four or five, with what seemed like parents and their teenage children.

After several open-air encounters someone in each group wanted a free Glow-Stick. The first group who took the test, four young ladies, ended up leaving before hearing the Good News, except one young lady who was convicted by what she heard. She thanked me for sharing with her as she goes to church but never heard it explained this way.

Joe, one of our sowers, asked her how did this message of looking at God's Ten Commandments applied to her affect her? She almost had tears in her eyes when see stated she was devasted and now understands what it means to REPENT of her sins, and just saying you believe in God wouldn't be enough.

Sad to say the other three groups who stopped also were pulled away, by the parents who were with them. When they heard that their child, children, were "Liars, Thieves, Blasphemer's, and Adulteries at heart, one parent stated that their child never would swear, using God's name in vain, that her daughter knew better then to do that. Yet when I confronted her with that question, asking her to be honest before a Holy God the young girl admitted she had, several times.

It is sad to see the parents drag these kids away from hearing the whole truth. It's sad that all they want to believe is that their kids are good, and yet even the parents are not good as God see's us. This is Satan at his best, deceiving others in this world to think that no matter what they do, the preaching is, that God is love and He would forgive them. Well this time it was Jacob who was willing to take the test to get a Glow-Stick for what looked like his girlfriend?

This young man was wearing a black rosary beads around his neck, against a bright red shirt. There were two younger girls and what appeared to be a mom with them. You should have seen how difficult it was for him in front of his peers, to answer four of the Commandments.

He laughed about lying, he put his head down about stealing, stated how everybody swears, but when asked about lust and what Jesus said it was the same as adultery, he started to blush, with head down and said it was hard not to.

He admitted to being guilty, but when I asked where would God have to send him, Heaven or Hell, both he and, (I'll call her mom) stated at the same time Heaven! I asked how could that be? They both said, "because God is a loving God". That's when I try to explain about breaking man's Law, what would a just Judge do and again mom says, heh! we have to go, and they all left.

A little while later Joe offered to buy me an ice cream at Sparky's which is right next to where we do our open air. Jacob and his family were inside and that's when I called his name out and told him to watch the silver napkin holder where I make a coin having the Ten Commandments on them appear. He was amazed and so was his girlfriend. She asked if I could get her one, and I did. That's when I explained about the 2nd Commandment about not having any Idols.

At this point he picked up the cross hanging on his neck and kissed it. Telling me how much he loved God. Again, I asked him to read the 2nd Commandment as we are not to have any Idols. That's when I asked what did the black beads mean that were all around his neck.

Do they represent Mary, that you pray her prayer ten times, then one Our Father, and then again ten times the Hail Mary? He then asked how did I know that, and I told him I used to do the same thing, as I was raised Catholic and believed like him and that's what we are supposed to do.

I then asked him if he heard that Mary was crying her eyes out in Heaven because everyone was praying to her instead of the One and only Begotten Son, Jesus the Christ. I gave him some more tracks and asked if he would read them as it may help him understand.

Now comes the amazing part, Brandt was doing an Open Air when Jason came by again. As he listened to what Brandt was saying, I noticed he was not wearing the black rosary beads anymore. I can only surmise that the Lord had opened his eyes and he understood the truth.

Pray Junior hears the WHOLE TRUTH

December 2011

Last Saturday night was quiet.

One of the several times I was offering a Glow-Stick for a prize to those who pass by, who could answer the question, "what was the original color of Coca Cola"? A man named Junior, who was with two young girls shouted out, "CLEAR". I thanked them for taking the time to answer but stated I'm sorry that's the wrong answer. I then encouraged them to continue to guess as I told them that there was no limit on how many guesses they could have. With that the girls started to shout our more colors. The youngest one shouted out, "GREEN". That's when I told her she had the correct answer and come and get her prize.

Seeing that they were young, the one who answered correctly was about ten and the other who was her sister was about 13, I asked the man who was with them if he was their father, he said no that he was their uncle.

That's when I asked if he would come to me and help with getting the prize for his nieces as I thought they were too young to answer the next question. He did and I proceeded to walk him through the GOOD PERSON test.

He was very direct with his answers and didn't try to justify or minimize his sins as most people who take the test do. After each question about lying, stealing, Blasphemy, and lust in his heart, he would look at his niece's and then his head would bow down, as he said, "YES"

When I asked if he would be innocent or guilty in reference to breaking God's Law's he immediately answered guilty! When I asked him where would God have to send him, Heaven or Hell, he put his head down and pointed to the ground.

Amazing how most who take this test have a difficult time using the word, "HELL." As I said he was very direct with his answers and when I asked if that concerned him, he stated, "YES". I then asked if he knew what God did for him so that he wouldn't have to go to Hell? He now raised he head and looked at me and stated, " He died on the cross."

That's when I ask who the he is, is it "Mohamed who died on the cross? " That's when he said no, Jesus. I then asked so based on what you just said all mankind is going to Heaven? Now with a twisted look on his face he said, "NO", that wouldn't make sense. That's when I asked what did he need to do now?

He shrugged his shoulders and said no. That's when I mentioned REPENT, that it was Jesus Himself who said in Luke 3:3,5 that unless you repent you will surely perish! I explained that it meant to having remorse, regret, a Godly sorrow for causing Jesus to go to cross.

He stated he hadn't done that hearing that way made him feel guilty about what he had done. I asked if he would like to do that now and again, he starred at his niece's and stated that he wasn't ready yet, but would think about what I said. He then put his hand out to thank me for getting him involved in the conversation.

I told him I would pray for him to ask the Lord tonight before he goes to sleep that he would ask for the Lord to reveal himself to him and to act on what he hears. As he was leaving, he took another Tract that we hand out, "Are You Good Enough to Go to Heaven?

Way of the Master Seminar with NEW Sowers

December 2011

The exciting part to me was that we had three new seed sowers, and one Pastor.

Wayne, who says he is 87, and being a Christian for over 50 years, was excited as he started to hand out the Million Dollar Gospel Tracts to those who passed by him. Catherine had explained it just like fishing, sometimes you get a bite and many times you don't, but at least you are being obedient to our Lord by given out God's Word to those who may never hear it.

Then Vittoria became involved as well. As she claimed how all the years of claiming Christ as her Lord she never shared with strangers. As with everything we do in life we must practice to learn how to make it easier and here's the big one, "More Comfortable"

Then we had Linda, this was her 2nd time on Mill with us. You should hear how excited she was to be there and listen to her tell us how during the week she was able to give away more Gospel Tracts. As she too has been born again for years and has been frustrated that she hasn't been able to share with those she meets on a regular basis. She told us how she gave one to her Doctor which was the first time she did something like that and was excited about it and know wanted to do even more.

Response from Pastor Nick: What a blessing Tom. God is powerfully at work and you are a wonderful example of obedience in spreading His Word. I really appreciated all of the Scripture that was referenced in supporting the need to present the Law as a means of pointing out our sinfulness and need for a Savior. I found the video on the issue of a false conversion sobering, convicting and helpful, as it practically presented the signs of a false conversion. We all need to do a better job of speaking the truth in love when presented with "fruit not consistent with repentance."

I believe that encouraging all in attendance to participate as "active observers" is a most important component. I was convicted by the intentional love demonstrated to the lost by those on your team.

Specifically, I noted that you so kindly passed out tracks with sincere enthusiasm to those walking by and you did not display any resentment toward those who rudely displayed their verbal and non-verbal disgust for the Lord. On two or three occasions I watched you as a crowd of people were drawn to you as you shared the Good Person Test with people while standing on the large sidewalk flower planter pot .

You showed Godly discernment as you needed to quickly to determine whom were possible hearers of the Word and whom were antagonists portraying themselves as interested persons. You showed real concern for those taking the test and were patient with them when they needed to ponder a question or rethink their response based on your follow- up questions. In the face of occasional hecklers, you politely continued your focus on the person you were engaging and did not become distracted. I believe it to be best stated that you were modeling walking in the Spirit.

Thank you and your team for putting on the seminar. I look forward to working with you in the future to hone my own skill in this area. so that I might do a better job daily reaching the lost. For His glory,

Nick D.

Pastor of Small Groups

Then there was our heckler? There was a guy in a cowboy hat singing on Mill Ave where we usually set up. We set up the banner that asks the question, "Are you a Good Person." In front of it I did some Open Air, giving away glow sticks to people who would take the Good Person Test.

This man for whatever reason decided to accuse me of horrendous crimes against women and using vulgarity to accentuate his point through his loud speaker that he was using when he was singing. I have learned to ignore those who speak with demonic possession, and focus on the ones who are in front of me who want to take the Good Person Test. By the way, this is a great way to draw a larger crowd as those who hear that kind of rhetoric are curious and they stop to listen.

Saturday Night in Tempe June 2012

This Saturday night like all the others, we were blessed to be able to publicly go out and share the Gospel of Jesus Christ, to those who may be lost.

My Worship Pastor Nathan and his teenage son Aaron, helped me set up the sign that asks if they can prove that they are a "Good Person?" If they can, they can get a free Glow-Stick. It's amazing how many claimed, they are GOOD. This is even authenticated in the Bible as it states, in Proverbs 20:6. ***"Most men will proclaim everyone his own goodness:"***

Buy asking them just four simple questions?

Ever lied

Stolen

Sworn

Looked with lust?

All say they have, but when asked if they would be innocent or guilty the majority say, INNOCENT!

What would you say?

Al, Dan, Nathan and even his teenage son Aaron are handing out probably 100's of Gospel Tracts in one night. This Tract uses the Law as well to convict them of their sin.

The Lord Himself stated, in Mark 16:15, "Go into all the world and preach the gospel to all creation, and then again in Acts 1:8," but you will receive power when the Holy Spirit has come upon you; and you shall be My witnesses, both in Jerusalem, (Phoenix) and in all Judea (Tempe) and Samaria, (Scottsdale) and even to the remotest part of the earth."(A little humor with the towns in the parentheses)

Experience the joy of knowing that you are being an obedient servant for the Lord. Jesus' prayer in (Luke 10:2) request us: "The harvest is plentiful, but the laborers are few; therefore, beseech the Lord of the harvest to send out laborers into His harvest.

Then in (John 14:15), "If you love Me, you will keep My commandments." You might want to read (John 15:14) as well. Below are pictures that Pastor Nathan took of those who stopped by to answer the Good Person Test to get a free Glow-Stick.

Here are those who pass by who wanted to take the Good Person Test to get a FREE Glow-Stick. I don't get it do you? It amazes me that men of all ages will take the time for the Good Person Test just to get a Glow-Stick. I praise the Lord for using me in reaching those who may be lost

A night at the Hospital

Tonight, was an amazing night. I got an email that a friend of ours 18-month old son, Addison was in the hospital. Catherine and I went to visit and found the boy improving...Praise God. We were able to share with several of the hospital staff including the volunteer person who escorted us to the room, as we gave her a Million Dollar Gospel Tract for taking us and explained that she needed to read the back to find out if she was GOOD enough to get into Heaven.

As we were leaving, I asked a man which way to go to get to the exit. He was kind enough to give us a long explanation of all the turns we needed to make. With that I gave him a million for being so helpful and then he stated that he would take us to where we needed to go. While walking I asked him who was he here for and he told me about his five-year old daughter who was in for over a month and had brain surgery removing a tumor.

Now at the door I showed him that a silver coin can appear from the chrome handles of a wheelchair, and gave it to him explaining that it was a commemorative coin and that it had the Ten Commandments on one side and the Gospel of Jesus Christ on the other. Then an amazing thing happened...he asked if I would come back with him to show what I just done to his daughter.

I looked at Catherine and we both said yes. When we got to the room the little girl was sleeping and several of the family members were there. So, at that point we gave each of them a Million Dollar Gospel Tract. The man's wife then asked if we could come back about an hour later as they would have to wake up their daughter to get her ready for before she would go to sleep for the night. With that request, how could we refuse, so we left to grab a quick bite and came back about an hour later.

The little girl was now awake but I could see she was sedated, but she did give us a slight hand wave to acknowledge our presence. I showed her the coin trick and placed it in her hand as she could barely raise her hand. The father and mother were very appreciative that we came back, so that's when I showed them the Red and Blue illusion cards again, in more detail. The wife was enamored on how her eyes where fooling her and then I walked her through the Law and the consequences of violating them. I summed up that all the religions in world were false representation of trying to get to Heaven.

Some religions pray to a priest to have them forgive them of their sins as I was once Catholic and that's what I was taught by them. But now my eyes have been opened and I know the truth. That's when I told them the only way that I can be accepted into the Heavenly Kingdom was that I needed to repent of my sins, lying, stealing, cursing, and lust to name a few, and place my trust in Jesus Christ alone to forgive me.

A nurse came in and we were going to leave, but that's when I was convicted that we needed to pray over this little girl and I asked her parents if it would be okay and asked them to come close to their daughter and we all laid hands on her and Catherine and I prayed.

Now comes the amazing part that Catherine and I got a kick out of. I hope you continue and don't stop reading yet. The father asked me what my name was as he really appreciated us being there. Now here it comes. You're going to love this...really, he said his name was Moses....Moses!

So now I can say I finally met Moses!

You can visit my site: **www.tillthenetsRFull.org**

Verses for Marriage Counseling

November 2012

Genesis 2:24 For this reason a man shall leave his father and his mother, and be joined to his wife; and they shall become one flesh.

Genesis 3:1-7 The Fall of Man

1 Now the serpent was craftier than any beast of the field which the Lord God had made. And he said to the woman, "Indeed, has God said, 'You shall not eat from any tree of the garden'?"

2 The woman said to the serpent, "From the fruit of the trees of the garden we may eat;

3 but from the fruit of the tree which is in the middle of the garden, God has said, 'You shall not eat from it or touch it, or you will die.'"

4 The serpent said to the woman, "You surely will not die!

5 For God knows that in the day you eat from it your eyes will be opened, and you will be like God, knowing good and evil."

6 When the woman saw that the tree was good for food, and that it was a delight to the eyes, and that the tree was desirable to make one wise, she took from its fruit and ate; and she gave also to her husband with her, and he ate.

7 Then the eyes of both of them were opened, and they knew that they were naked; and they sewed fig leaves together and made themselves loin coverings.

Matthew 6:14-15 For if you forgive others for their transgressions, your heavenly Father will also forgive you. 15 But if you do not forgive others, then your Father will not forgive your transgressions.

Luke 6:27-29 "But I say to you who listen, love your enemies, do good to those who hate you, 28 bless those who curse you, pray for those who mistreat you. 29 Whoever hits you on the cheek, offer him the other also; and whoever takes away your coat, do not withhold your shirt from him either.

Luke 6:46 Builders and Foundations
"Why do you call Me, 'Lord, Lord,' and do not do what I say?

John 13:34-35 A new commandment I give to you, that you love one another, even as I have loved you, that you also love one another.

John 13:35 By this all men will know that you are My disciples, if you have love for one another."

John 14:15 "If you love Me, you will keep My commandments. Interesting how John 15:14 states:

You are My friends if you do what I command you.

John 14:21 He who has My commandments and keeps them is the one who loves Me; and he who loves Me will be loved by My Father, and I will love him and will disclose Myself to him."

John 15:10 If you keep My commandments, you will abide in My love; just as I have kept My Father's commandments and abide in His love.

John 15:12-14 "This is My commandment, that you love one another, just as I have loved you. 13 Greater love has no one than this, that one lay down his life for his friends. 14 You are My friends if you do what I command you.

Romans 15:1-7 Self-denial on Behalf of Others Now we who are strong ought to bear the weaknesses of those without strength and not just please ourselves. 2 Each of us is to please his neighbor for his good, to his edification. 3 For even Christ did not please Himself; but as it is written, "The reproaches of those who reproached You fell on ME." 4 For whatever was written in earlier times was written for our instruction, so that through perseverance and the encouragement of the Scriptures we might have hope. 5 Now may the God who gives perseverance and encouragement grant you to be of the same mind with one another according to Christ Jesus, 6 so that with one accord you may with one voice glorify the God and Father of our Lord Jesus Christ. 7 Therefore, accept one another, just as Christ also accepted us to the glory of God.

Ephesians 4:25-32 Therefore, laying aside falsehood, speak truth each one of you with his neighbor, for we are members of one another. 26 BE angry, and yet do not sin; do not let the sun go down on your anger, 27 and do not give the devil an opportunity. 29 Let no unwholesome word proceed from your mouth, but only such a word as is good for edification according to the need of the moment, so that it will give grace to those who hear. 30 Do not grieve the Holy Spirit of God, by whom you were sealed for the day of redemption. 31 Let all bitterness and wrath and anger and clamor and slander be put away from you, along with all malice. 32 Be kind to one another, tender-hearted, forgiving each other, just as God in Christ also has forgiven you.

Ephesians 5:1-5 Be Imitators of God Therefore, be imitators of God, as beloved children; 2 and walk in love, just as Christ also loved you and gave Himself up for us, an offering and a sacrifice to God as a fragrant aroma. 3 But immorality or any impurity or greed must not even be named among you, as is proper among saints; 4 and there must be no filthiness and silly talk, or coarse jesting, which are not fitting, but rather giving of thanks. 5 For this you know with certainty, that no immoral or impure person or covetous man, who is an idolater, has an inheritance in the kingdom of Christ and God.

Ephesians 5:22-31 Marriage Like Christ and the Church Wives, be subject to your own husbands, as to the Lord. 23 For the husband is the head of the wife, as Christ also is the head of the church, He Himself being the Savior of the body. 24 But as the church is subject to Christ, so also the wives ought to be to their husbands in everything. 25 Husbands, love your wives, just as Christ also loved the church and gave Himself up for her, 26 so that He might sanctify her, having cleansed her by the washing of water with the word, 27 that He might present to Himself the church in all her glory, having no spot or wrinkle or any such thing; but that she would be holy and blameless. 28 So husbands ought also to love their own wives as their own bodies. He who loves his own wife loves himself; 29 for no one ever hated his own flesh, but nourishes and cherishes it, just as Christ also does the church, 30 because we are members of His body. 31 For this reason A man shall leave his father and mother and shall be joined to his wife, and the two shall become one flesh.

Ephesians 5:33 Nevertheless, each individual among you also is to love his own wife even as himself, and the wife must see to it that she respects her husband.

Ephesians 6:1-2 Family Relationships Children, obey your parents in the Lord, for this is right. 2 Honor your father and mother (which is the first commandment with a promise),

2 Timothy 2:24-26 The Lord's bond- servant must not be quarrelsome, but be kind to all, able to teach, patient when wronged, 25 with gentleness correcting those who are in opposition, if perhaps God may grant them repentance leading to the knowledge of the truth, 26 and they may come to their senses and escape from the snare of the devil, having been held captive by him to do his will.

Hebrews 3:13-14 But encourage one another day after day, as long as it is still called "Today," so that none of you will be hardened by the deceitfulness of sin. 14 For we have become partakers of Christ, if we hold fast the beginning of our assurance firm until the end,

Hebrews 10:26-30 Christ or Judgment For if we go on sinning willfully after receiving the knowledge of the truth, there no longer remains a sacrifice for sins, 27 but a terrifying expectation of judgment and the fury of A fire which will consume the adversaries. 28 Anyone who has set aside the Law of Moses dies without mercy on the testimony of two or three witnesses. 29 How much severer punishment do you think he will deserve who has trampled underfoot the Son of God, and has regarded as unclean the blood of the covenant by which he was sanctified, and has insulted the Spirit of grace? 30 For we know Him who said,
"***Vengeance is Mine, I will repay." And again,***
"The Lord will judge His people."

1 Peter 3:1-12 Godly Living. In the same way, you wives, be submissive to your own husbands so that even if any of them are disobedient to the word, they may be won without a word by the behavior of their wives, 2 as they observe your chaste and respectful behavior. 3 Your adornment must not be merely external—braiding the hair, and wearing gold jewelry, or putting on dresses; 4 but let it be the hidden person of the heart, with the imperishable quality of a gentle and quiet spirit, which is precious in the sight of God. 5 For in this way in former times the holy women also, who hoped in God, used to adorn themselves, being submissive to their own husbands; 6 just as Sarah obeyed Abraham, calling him lord, and you have become her children if you do what is right without being frightened by any fear. 7 You husbands in the same way, live with your wives in an understanding way, as with someone weaker, since she is a woman; and show her honor as a fellow heir of the grace of life, so that your prayers will not be hindered. 8

To sum up, all of you be harmonious, sympathetic, brotherly, kindhearted, and humble in spirit; 9 not returning evil for evil or insult for insult, but giving a blessing instead; for you were called for the very purpose that you might inherit a blessing.

10 "THE ONE WHO DESIRES LIFE, TO LOVE AND SEE GOOD DAYS, MUST KEEP HIS TONGUE FROM EVIL AND HIS LIPS FROM SPEAKING DECEIT.11 "HE MUST TURN AWAY FROM EVIL AND DO GOOD; HE MUST SEEK PEACE AND PURSUE IT.12 "FOR THE EYES OF THE LORD ARE TOWARD THE RIGHTEOUS, AND HIS EARS ATTEND TO THEIR PRAYER, BUT THE FACE OF THE LORD IS AGAINST THOSE WHO DO EVIL."

1 Peter 4:8-11 Above all, keep fervent in your love for one another, because love covers a multitude of sins. 9 Be hospitable to one another without complaint. 10 As each one has received a special gift, employ it in serving one another as good stewards of the manifold grace of God. 11 Whoever speaks, is to do so as one who is speaking the utterances of God; whoever serves is to do so as one who is serving by the strength which God supplies; so that in all things God may be glorified through Jesus Christ, to whom belongs the glory and dominion forever and ever. Amen.

2 Peter 1:4-15 For by these He has granted to us His precious and magnificent promises, so that by them you may become partakers of the divine nature, having escaped the corruption that is in the world by lust. 5 Now for this very reason also, applying all diligence, in your faith supply moral excellence, and in your moral excellence, knowledge, 6 and in your knowledge, self- control, and in your self- control, perseverance, and in your perseverance, godliness, 7 and in your godliness, brotherly kindness, and in your brotherly kindness, love. 8 For if these qualities are yours and are increasing, they render you neither useless nor unfruitful in the true knowledge of our Lord Jesus Christ. 9 For he who lacks these qualities is blind or short- sighted, having forgotten his purification from his former sins. 10 Therefore, brethren, be all the more diligent to make certain about His calling and choosing you; for as long as you practice these things, you will never stumble; 11 for in this way the entrance into the eternal kingdom of our Lord and Savior Jesus Christ will be abundantly supplied to you. 12 Therefore, I will always be ready to remind you of these things, even though you *already* know *them,* and have been established in the truth which is present with *you.* 13 I consider it right, as long as I am in this *earthly* dwelling, to stir you up by way of reminder, 14 knowing that the laying aside of my *earthly* dwelling is imminent, as also our Lord Jesus Christ has made clear to me. 15And I will also be diligent that at any time after my departure you will be able to call these things to mind.

1John 3:1-24

(1) See how great a love the Father has bestowed on us, that we would be called children of God; and *such* we are.

For this reason, the world does not know us, because it did not know Him.

(2) Beloved, now we are children of God, and it has not appeared as yet what we will be. We know that when He appears, we will be like Him, because we will see Him just as He is.

(3) And everyone who has this hope fixed on Him purifies himself, just as He is pure.

(4) Everyone who practices sin also practices lawlessness; and sin is lawlessness.

(5) You know that He appeared in order to take away sins; and in Him there is no sin.

(6) No one who abides in Him sins; no one who sins has seen Him or knows Him.

(7) Little children, make sure no one deceives you; the one who practices righteousness is righteous, just as He is righteous;

(8) the one who practices sin is of the devil; for the devil has sinned from the beginning. The Son of God appeared for this purpose, to destroy the works of the devil.

(9) No one who is born of God practices sin, because His seed abides in him; and he cannot sin, because he is born of God.

(10) By this the children of God and the children of the devil are obvious: anyone who does not practice righteousness is not of God, nor the one who does not love his brother.

(11) For this is the message which you have heard from the beginning, that we should love one another;

(12) not as Cain, who was of the evil one and slew his brother. And for what reason did he slay him? Because his deeds were evil, and his brothers were righteous.

(13) Do not be surprised, brethren, if the world hates you.

(14) We know that we have passed out of death into life, because we love the brethren. He who does not love abides in death.

(15) Everyone who hates his brother is a murderer; and you know that no murderer has eternal life abiding in him.

(16) We know love by this, that He laid down His life for us; and we ought to lay down our lives for the brethren.

(17) But whoever has the world's goods, and sees his brother in need and closes his heart against him, how does the love of God abide in him?

(18) Little children, let us not love with word or with tongue, but with deed and truth.

(19) We will know by this that we are of the truth, and will assure our heart before Him

(20) in whatever our heart condemns us; for God is greater than our heart and knows all things.

(21) Beloved, if our heart does not condemn us, we have confidence before God;

(22) and whatever we ask we receive from Him, because we keep His commandments and do the things that are pleasing in His sight.

(23) This is His commandment, that we believe in the name of His Son Jesus Christ, and love one another, just as He commanded us.

(24) The one who keeps His commandments abides in Him, and He in him. We know by this that He abides in us, by the Spirit whom He has given us.

Jude 1:17-23 Keep Yourselves in the Love of God 17 But you, beloved, ought to remember the words that were spoken beforehand by the apostles of our Lord Jesus Christ, 18 that they were saying to you, " In the last time there will be mockers, following after their own ungodly lusts." 19 These are the ones who cause divisions, worldly- minded, devoid of the Spirit. 20 But you, beloved, building yourselves up on your most holy faith, praying in the Holy Spirit, 21 keep yourselves in the love of God, waiting anxiously for the mercy of our Lord Jesus Christ to eternal life. 22 And have mercy on some, who are doubting; 23 save others, snatching them out of the fire; and on some have mercy with fear, hating even the garment polluted by the flesh.

Believers Receive the Holy Spirit the moment they are Born-Again… Saved!

(John 3:3-6, Romans 8:9-11,
1stCorinthians 3:16-17, 1st John 4:2,13)

My Testimony Easter Sunday March 2013

The following was the information I gave at Cactus Christian Fellowship in Phoenix AZ.

Here are three situations where I believe that Lord Jesus the Christ was trying to get my attention.

1. The first one was when working with a company that had people there who were predominately Mormons. This would be the last time they brought up what they believed, as they asked me if I knew the answer to three questions which only all Mormons know? I asked what were they? they stated.

    1) We know where we came from,
    2) We know where we are,
    3) We know where we are going.

    Without hesitation I responded, being raised as a Catholic I knew the answer to those questions. I told them I came from my mother, I'm here in Arizona and I'm going to Hell. They never brought up anything again about their religion!

2. The second was receiving this book, "More Than I Carpenter" after attending a sales convention in Las Vegas, hosted by a realtor named Tom Hopkins.

    A few months before Aril 3rd 1994 Tom Hopkins mailed me the book, "More than a Carpenter." When I received it at my office, I threw behind me on my credence, as I knew who Christ was. A friend of mine who was down the hall from my office came and saw the book on my credenza and stated, "I didn't know you were a Christian?" I yelled back, "I'm not a Christian I'm a Catholic!" He then stated he was sorry and never brought it up again.

3. Then finally the third one was me meeting a gorgeous blond named, Lanaye! This encounter was the most important one. I volunteered to help at the tennis event in Scottsdale AZ. Every day this attractive woman came and I escorted her to her seat. Couldn't resist that on the last day of the tournament I asked her if she would go out with me for lunch. She stated that she was a Christian, and only would go with me if I first would take her to hear her Pastor on the following Sunday, which happened to be Easter Sunday.

That was the day I was saved, April 3rd 1994.

Here comes the rest of the story!

After my conversion, I tried sharing with my older sister and brother and was told if I keep talking about Jesus, I'm no longer welcome in the family.

During the next year the six salesman who were working for me all started their own agency, including my nephew who took two of my secretaries with him.

Belonging to a Tennis club, I shared with them what happened to me and because of that, I was no longer invited to compete in tournaments.

Years later after hearing a man called Ray Comfort and reading this Scripture and 1st Corinthians 1:18 opened my eyes. Here's what it states: Verse 18, "For the preaching of the cross is to them that perish foolishness; but unto us which are saved it is the power of God."

If I was told that I needed to accepted Jesus in my life to have a better life, I'm pretty sure, I would have gone back to where I'd had come from because it was a whole lot better.

It took about three years for me to want to get Baptized as I knew I had been Baptized as a baby. Standing up in front of about two thousand people and telling them why, was at that time, fearful.

Several years later the Holy Spirit convicted me that watching pornography was wrong. I justified it because of my age how many times I had done it…no big deal. At that moment, I realized that it was wrong it was as if I was having an adulterous affair against Catherine. I asked the Lord to forgive me and called Catherine into the room so she could see what I was watching. After reviving her from fainting… kidding, I asked her to forgive me and would she pray for me that God would take that desire away and have me hate that sin as much as He does. That prayer had been answered. Here are a few more of what the Lord may want you to hear!

2 Cor. 7:10. For Godly sorrow produces a repentance that lead to salvation

Romans 8:9 However, you are not in the flesh but in the Spirit, if indeed the Spirit of God dwells in you. But if anyone does not have the Spirit of Christ, he does not belong to Him.

1st Corinthians 6:19-20 Or do you not know that your body is a temple of the Holy Spirit who is in you, whom you have from God, and that you are not your own? 20 For you have been bought with a price: therefore, glorify God in your body.

2nd Cor.5:17 Therefore, if anyone is in Christ, he is a new creation. The old has passed away; behold, the new has come.

1st Friday Night at the Phoenix Art Fair
April 2013

Writing this, I thought of those of you who attended the March 23rd Way of the Master Seminar.

The reason I host this seminar is to help those who claim Christ as Lord and want to serve Him for the eternal gift of Salvation He still is providing. One of the greatest gifts we can give our Lord Jesus is to answer His prayer, in Luke 10:2.

What a blessing to have almost all who attended come out either last Saturday or last night to watch as we put into practice this Biblical principal shown at the seminar. What a joy to see Nathan, our Worship Pastor as this was his first time out with us. With us this night were Keith, Steve, Reese, and Patrick who brought his 11-yr. old son Joey were there as well.

This night was packed, I mean packed with lost souls who gathered in large groups in front of me, as I offered them a chance to receive a free Glow-Stick if they could prove they were a Good Person. This was the first time I gave away over 60 Glow-Sticks. I also know the team gave away 100's of Gospel Tracts.

Slowly the Lord's prayer in Luke 10:2 is being answered. Keith who attended his first seminar March of 2012 has now several times found the courage through the Holy Spirit to stand on the box and draw crowds by offering them a FREE Glow-Stick if they can pass the Good Person Test

Couldn't more of us do the same by answering Jesus' prayer?

Here is Jesus' prayer in Luke 10:2

And he said to them, "The harvest is plentiful, but the laborers are few. Therefore, pray earnestly to the Lord of the harvest to send out laborers into his harvest.

Sad, as many who take the test claim to be a Christian, come up with reasons that God would not send any one to Hell because He is Love, He forgives. Or one said she was baptized, another stated they have purgatory, others say they know Jesus, some state they believe in Jesus.

They can't accept a God of Justice who in John 3:18, states His Wrath is upon them, they have only been told of His Love. It's true He is Loving and because of it, He must punish those who have not repented and placed their trust in Jesus Christ ALONE! Nothing else will save them.

He lowered Himself being human, suffered the horrific torture at the hands of the Roman soldiers, nailed to a cross to take the penalty for those of us who admit being law breakers and should have been punished ourselves.

2nd Corinthians 7:10 makes it clear: For the sorrow that is according to *the will of* God produces a repentance without regret, leading to salvation, but the sorrow of the world produces death. (NASB)

Now going out every Saturday night and prayerfully the 1st Friday of each month, to reach out to the lost. The Lord willing, you'll find the time to do something like this as well.

1st Friday on 3rd and Roosevelt

And an EXCITING Sunday May 2013

Catherine and I rode down with Keith, and his daughter Kate, to 1st Friday Night at 3rd and Roosevelt to share the Gospel.

A little while later a first timer, Tony and his wife Lorna, met us there. We all go to Harvest Bible Chapel. As usual Friday night at the Phoenix Art Fair was swarming with thousands of people. Right after we set up the banner that asks the question: "ARE YOU A GOOD PERSON?", they can get a free Glow-Stick if they are.

Immediately a crowd was in front of me willing to prove they were good. About ten minutes into asking them about violating God's Ten Commandments, the police stopped me because I was drawing a crowd that always comes when I offer a free Glow-Stick to anyone who can prove they are a good person.

I've been on the triangle every 1st Friday of the month, which is on the corner of 3rd and Roosevelt, for over four years. I was told it was a hazard for me to do that because the crowd would block the sidewalk and others would have to walk on the street. At this triangle there is yellow tape that extends out from the sidewalk about three feet that allows pedestrians to walk on the street safely. Really!!! I don't get it, do you?

We then went across the street where we set up the sign again. Praise the Lord as that side provided more listeners and better lightning that ever before! Catherine came to me shocked and asked if I had any more Million Dollar Gospel Tracts, as she had given away over 200 of them. She was shocked as it was only 9:30PM!

We were met by others who want to reach out to the lost. Patrick, and his wife Vinka and their young son Joey, as well as his Pastor from North Phoenix Baptist Church. Matt, Leigh, and Matthew were there as well.

Now comes the exciting Sunday!

After worship Catherine and I went to Denny's to get a bite to eat. An elderly couple was struggling to get out of their car. The man was out of the car and on crutches and the woman was trying to get out, to reach her walker. I walked over to lend a hand. As they followed us in, I turned and gave her a Million Dollar Gospel Tract for allowing me to help her. She gave me a big smile and thanked me! As Catherine and I were about to open the door, her husband asked if I was a Christian. I asked him why he asked that and he said I gave them a Gospel Tract. That's when his wife said we've been believers for over 50 years and can't remember anyone giving us a Gospel Tract. They sat with us at Denny's and were able to hear how I use the Law to share with those who serve us at restaurants.

I always ask this question after we give our order to our server. "We usually pray before we eat is that okay with you?" They always say yes. Then I ask them, "Is there anything that we can pray for you about?" This time I was pleasantly surprised as Catherine beat me to it! This is when I wish I had a camera as you should have seen the joyful look our servers face! She told us that she needed to take a test so that she could go to nursing school and was concerned about doing it.

She came back several times while we were eating to ask if we needed anything else. That's when I will bring out the Red and Blue illusion card which helps them realize that their eyes can fool them and then I can proceed to ask them about breaking God's Ten Commandants. Interestingly enough she stayed to answer the four specific questions about lying, stealing, swearing and lust. She was truly convicted by her own answers and that God would have no choice but to send her to Hell.

Thankfully this concerned her, as many times those who admit to being law breakers believe God is love and would not punish them. Now comes the part we all love! Yadi, our waitress, turned to me and asked, "So what do I have to do to be saved?" Praise the Lord as I could see a contrite heart at that moment!

I explained to her she should go home and get on her knees and ask God for forgiveness and REPENT, which meant having Godly sorrow and that she would now place her TRUST in Jesus Christ alone for the forgiveness of her sins. That's when I shared with her what it would be like to be born again, as that's what happens. We are given the Holy Spirit and that's what transforms us from the inside out. I asked if she had a Bible at home and she said she did so I told her to read it her obey what it says, as the Word of God should not be read like a novel but as a love letter with instruction on what our Heavenly Father requires from those whom He has adopted into His Kingdom.

Here's a side note. While we were eating, a man who was sitting across from us got up to leave and told me that I had dropped some money under the table. I bent down to retrieve it and immediately offered it to him for being honest enough to tell me. You should have seen the look on his face as he reluctantly took it, and I told him to read the back, as now he had the Million Dollar Gospel Tract.

So, as she is pondering her faith, she goes to serve others and then a little while later bring another waitress who had just lost her infant nine-month-old grandson. This lady wanted to know if it was okay to scream at God in anger. After expressing our remorse for her loss, she mentioned what a good person she was and why would God do that?

That's when I asked her if she would answer a few questions to see if she was GOOD? Sadly, she didn't believe in Hell or even Heaven! That's when I looked at her and was amazed, that she would get angry at a God she doesn't even believe in.

Just as Yadi was going to serve another customer, before leaving our table, she said she was very appreciative about what I shared with her as she finally understood what she needs to do.

As we are writing this, Catherine stated, "It's good that we go out to eat so that we can engage with those who serve us so we can ask if we could pray for them. If we hadn't gone out after church today, we would have missed this tremendous opportunity to share."

It's amazing, after reading what the Lord Himself is asking for us to do for Him, by answering to His prayer.

" The harvest is plentiful, but the laborers are few; therefore, beseech the Lord of the harvest to send out laborers into His harvest." You can find it in two places (Luke 10:2, Matthew 9:37-38)(NASB)

Thomas Fusco Post from my Blog

June 2013

I had just finished ordering a cup of coffee at McDonald's register; when I backed away, I felt something hit my leg, and as I turned it was a little boy about three years old.

I bent down and handed him a Ten Commandment Coin. He immediately reached out for it and smiled. I now stepped to the side away from cash register to wait. A man came forward and said here's your coin back.

With that I told him it was free gift for his son. Now comes the exiting part, as I was now able to proclaim the Lord's name to a large group of people, in a public place. I told the man in a moderately raised voice, "It's a commemorative coin with the Ten Commandments on one side and the Gospel of Jesus Christ on the other. He thanked me and left with his tray of food.

I was then given my coffee and looked for a place to sit as I mentioned it was busy. I went into the children's area and saw him sitting with two other young boys. I approached him and stated that I was sorry as I didn't know he had other children as it wasn't fair that his brothers didn't get one. I gave one to the middle aged one and then asked what looked like the oldest, how old he was. He stated, ten. I then asked him to look at my hand and did he see anything, he replied no. So that's when the coin cones out of my hand. You should have seen the look on his face as he first stared at his father with wide eyes and then back to me with his mouth wide open.

He reached out for it and that's when I told the young boy that I give coins to children and Million Dollar Gospel Tracts to the parents, should I give one to his dad?

He immediately said yes, so I turned to the father and gave him one and stated that, of course it's not real but he needs to read the back as it's worth more than a Million.

Latter as I finished my coffee, I noticed that the man was sitting by himself facing out of the booth, no children present as they were probably playing on the slides, intently reading the Million Dollar Gospel Tract.

I tell you this story not because I did it but because it's what the Lord requires of ALL those who claim Him as Lord, to reach out to the lost; those who cross our paths on a daily basis. (Mark 16:15, Acts 1:8, Acts 4:10) to name a few. This is so simple and well received by those who get them. Please, please don't be like those I've meet over the years who attend church and because their Pastors' who tell them it's not how to share, as the people will throw them away.

PLEASE BELIEVE ME, THAT'S NOT TRUE!

The truth is the Word will never return void. With this new technology, the Million Dollar Gospel Tracts, you'd be able to place the Word of God into a stranger's hand. Don't you think this would be pleasing to God? It's in the Bible as well that the Angels in Heaven rejoice over one sinner who repents?

Saturday Night Live

June 2013

This Saturday night was a mix of every religious belief you can imagine.

As Al and I were driving down to Mill Ave in Tempe he mentioned that tonight was going to be demonic because the moon was 13% brighter than normal. It certainly proved to be just that!

Nathan, his son Aaron and his nephew Brandon were already on the corner there. These teens are a big help, as they help me set up The Good Person Test sign and sometime offer those who walk by the Million Dollar Gospel Tract.

I offer these Glow-Sticks as a prize to those who pass by if they can prove to me, they are a Good Person. They are very effective in attracting all kinds of people.

After doing several tests to those whose belief went from not believing in any God to those who did believe in the God but NOT of the Christian Bible to those who claimed they accepted Jesus but didn't call themselves Christians.

This couple came up to me after about an hour of giving many Glow-Sticks away to those who claimed they were good. age Once they admit what specific Laws they broke and show that are destined for Hell, I then give the saving Grace that can only come from Jesus' death and resurrection on the cross.

I mention this first as this was why this couple came to talk to me, as the man stated he appreciated what I was saying as he had accepted Jesus and never heard it that way before.

She told me that he was a changed man because of Jesus, as he was a drinker and she told him she would not marry a man who gets drunk. He smiled and stated that he accepted Jesus and he stopped drinking and he was now a changed man. He then made the comment that they don't go to Church or call themselves Christians.

At first, I thought they now had the truth but after hearing his last statement, I felt obligated to take him through the Commandments, to see if he really was saved, or just as many do think that Jesus was someone he just needed to accept.

Here is when I asked him if he thought he was a Good Person. He answered the questions quickly about him lying, stealing, swearing and lust in his heart, and stated he would be guilty like everyone else. (This is what they do, they like to place themselves in the same boat with all of mankind, so not be any different, and not really think themselves guilty) But because he changed, he would be okay with God.

That's when I was able to tell him that there's only one way anyone can get into Heaven. That is to REPENT and TRUST in Jesus Christ alone, not just because he stopped drinking, in other words him improving his life, but for what Jesus did for him and me on that cross. Jesus paid the fine for the crimes that he and I committed!

I explained what (Ephesians 2:8-9), states it's about Grace from God, not of works it's a free gift, so that no one can boast. Both he and his wife now had a true picture of what it's like for one to be Born Again. They both thanked me as what they were now hearing made sense! Praise the Lord for sending that couple to me so that the Lord could adopt another into the Kingdom (Ephesians 1:5)

Here are just two quotes from Charles Spurgeon on this subject:

Charles Spurgeon stated: Aim for REPENTANCE, God doesn't want STILL BORNS!

My Favorite: "I do not believe that any man can preach the gospel who does not preach Law. The Law is the needle, and you cannot draw the silken tread of the gospel through a man's heart until you first send the Law to make way for it.

My Birthday at McDonalds PV Mall

July 2013

$\mathcal{A}$nother Glorious encounter for the Lord! I'm so thankful that my Worship Pastor Nathan from Cactus Christian Fellowship asked these men if it would be okay if he took their picture, as this was his first-time meeting with us. This was after they stood for about 15 minutes taking the Good Person Test.

These three were kind enough to give me a light for the cake that my good friend Steve brought to celebrate my birthday during our Friday morning breakfast Bible study. They were heading towards the door when I shouted out and asked if any of them had a match as I needed one to light the candle on my birthday cake.

Well the one in the middle, Antonia, changed direction and headed back towards me with a cigarette lighter in hand. When the candle was lit, I offered the Million Dollar Gospel Tract and then saw the other two heading towards us and gave two more to give to them.

That's when the excitement started. Pastor Nathan stated he wanted to sing happy birthday and I then asked if they would sing with my friends, and they did!!! I then asked if they could guess my age and showed them a few of the Ten Commandment coins I always carry. They tried but failed miserably, they guessed way to low (45, then 50, 55). When I told them, I was 70 they wouldn't believe it. I told them that because it was my birthday and they didn't win the coin, I wanted them to have it anyway.

That's when I explained what it is. It's a commemorative coin with the Ten Commandments on one side and the Gospel of Jesus Christ on the other. They all smiled and thanked me. That's when I feel I can ask the tough question. Do you realize that we all are going to be judged by them one day, do you know what they are? By asking each one of them, one at a time, did they ever lie, steal, swear, or look with lust; they at first laughed and then became somber.

The one who is standing over me, Vincent, stated that he had never heard it explained like that before. He said now his mind is thinking about what could happen to him next. He stated he never even thought of it. But now it's on his mind and he'll be thinking about it all day... Praise the Lord!

It's awesome to watch the Holy Spirit convict those whom He chooses by allowing the WHOLE TRUTH of the God's Word being presented. This Biblical principle of using God's Law to open up a dialogue with the lost is, and I pray you see this, VERY SUCCESSFUL. As it makes them look examine themselves as to how God would see them, instead of me accusing them of being a sinner, by stating that they need Jesus.

Please pray for Vincent that his heart be broken for what he has done and accept the fact that he is headed for Hell. Pray that he sees the need to Repent and Trust (2nd Cor. 7:10) in the Lord Jesus the Christ for the forgiveness of his sin, so he can be set free from the Wrath of God. (John 3:36) Pray also the other two as well as they heard but… not were yet not convicted.

This Morning's at McDonald's 32nd and Shea

July 2013

This morning was another God given opportunity to present the TRUE Gospel to those who pass us by on a regular basis. Pastor Nathan and I were leaving McDonald's after having a joyful breakfast and as I was going to the counter to get a refill I heard loud talking coming just to the right of the door.

I asked if this was a party, and the one standing wearing the hat told me it was his birthday. With that I congratulated him and told him that mine was Sunday. He then asked if I would sing Happy Birthday to him and without hesitation I did. Fortunately, Nathan took this picture.

That's when he received a gift from me, several Million Dollar Gospel Tracts and I told him to give the rest to his friends. He stated no that now he was going to keep them as he is rich! I then told him he should give them to his friends just like I gave them to him and that he and his friends read the back as the message is worth more than a Million. Funny as now he asked me what else do you have for me? I then showed him how a silver coin could appear out of thin air and gave it to him explaining that it has the Ten Commandments on one side and the Gospel of Jesus Christ on the other.

Now you have to understand I have a hearing problem and have been told by many that I speak louder than I need to. So, with all of his friends listening as well as those sitting nearby, they hear the same salvation message as well. How awesome is that! In a fast food restaurant proclaiming the TRUE Gospel of Jesus Christ to many people at one time. Remember, I had to initiate this by asking the group what was going on and having several Million Dollar Gospel Tracts on me to spark their interest.

That's when I state that how sad it is that one day all of us could be judged by them and most people today don't even know them. He stated he did, so I said go ahead and name them I'll give you $20.00, you have 30 seconds. He could only name three as his mouth opened but nothing came out after the 3rd one. Funny how when those who claim they can become humbled when they realize they can't.

This is when I asked if I could help him and asked if he had ever told a lie, he said smiling, "YES". I asked what they call those who tell lies. He said. Steelers. I told him no that's Pittsburg Steelers the football team; he laughed and then stated a, "LIAR". I asked had he ever stolen anything and he put his head down and immediately stated that he was going to Hell. That's when I asked if that concerned him and he said, "YES"

I then asked if he knew what God a done for him so that he wouldn't have to go to Hell and he said, "He died on the Cross" That's when I stated that based on what he just said everyone on planet Earth would be going to

Heaven and yet he himself admitted he would be going to Hell because of his sinful lifestyle.

That's when they get to hear the truth of Salvation. That they need to Repent, sin no more, HATE the sin as much as God does and place their Trust in Jesus Christ alone, as an example, not what they do, give to the poor, go to Church, feed the homeless, but only what Jesus Christ has already done for us on that Cross, (Ephesians. 2:8-9) says it clearly! It's by faith alone it's a gift from God so that no one can boast! Maybe we shouldn't be waiting for them to come to us to ask "what do I have to do to get into Heaven?" You'll find the answer in (Luke: 18:18-27)

Last Night! What a Blessing from the Lord!

August 2013

Those of us who came out to the street corner of 3rd Ave and Roosevelt in Phoenix Art Fair.

My loving wife Catherine, our Worship Pastor Nathan and my good friend Keith, as well as Patrick and his 11-year-old son Joey. The streets again were full of people going whom I do not know, as they sometimes pass by us two or three times. It truly amazes me how many will stop by to receive a free Glow-Stick. Neither the age nor the sexual orientation matters, as many will stop by to get one and many times there are many groups as well.

Just think of the opportunity to bring them to their knees as they engage in taking the Good Person Test. The majority claim they are GOOD…just like the scripture states. "Most men will proclaim each his own goodness but, who can find a faithful man?" (Proverbs 20:6)

We had several one to many conversations about why, based on their answers to just four of God's Ten Commands they would be destined to Hell. It truly is sad to hear all the made-up reasons why God would not send anyone to Hell. Even those who claim to be Christian's state God is love and wouldn't send anyone to Hell.

SAD ISN'T IT!

The one encounter that was heartbreaking at first to me was a man who had admitted smashing a hammer to the head of another person and spent ten years in jail for it. Now out and living on the streets he admitted several times accepting Jesus but still continued in sin, and being human it would always be like that. I again explained that Jesus had already paid the fine for his crimes and if he had truly repented and placed his trust in Jesus for that, then he would be free from the torment that he was going through.

That's when he stated that he himself had to take care of those sins as no one else could do it for him. That's when I explained that he was still being held captive by Satan and I needed to give him what the Scripture says about that Ephesians 2:8-10, is very clear! "For by **grace** you have been saved through faith, and that **not of yourselves**; it is the **gift of God, not of works,** lest anyone should boast. For we are His workmanship, created in Christ Jesus for good works, which God prepared beforehand that we should walk in them."

There it was, A FREE GIFT! Just like why I gave him the Glow-Stick. He accepted he wasn't GOOD, but I gave it to him anyway. He started to understand and now comes a blessing from the Lord. I told him he needed to Repent and place his Trust in Jesus the Christ for the forgiveness of his sins, not what he does, but what Jesus already had done for him.

He now responded with his head down, his speech broken. That's when I felt to ask him if he wanted to do that now. He just nodded his head, I then told him to get on his knees and ask the Lord to forgive him and that from now on he would place his trust in what Jesus had done for him. As you see on the next page he got on his knees. That's when I laid my hands on him and prayed for him to receive the Holy Spirit and that the evil spirits and demons would no longer hold him captive in the precious name of Jesus the Christ.

I guess you would have had to have been there to see the peaceful look on his face when he stood up. With gratitude he took more of our written material and thanked me for being out on the street sharing the Lord with him. Leaving, he turned and stated he had never heard it that way before!

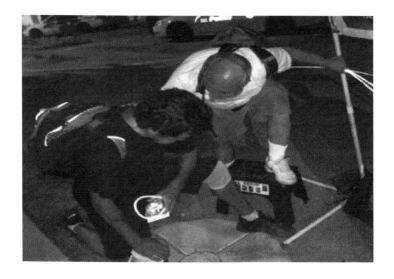

Not done yet as Joey, the 11-year-old had been asking me if he could get up on the box and use my microphone. Well what do you say to a child who is persistent? I got down, placed the microphone on him gave him a few Glow-Sticks and within seconds he started shouting out as I had,

"ANYONE WANT A FREE GLOW-STICK?"

Well after a few groups passed him a few stopped and stated they would like one. They asked what do I have to do to get one? Without hesitation he responded with, "You have to take the Good Person Test. Would you consider yourself to be a good person" Well the rest was amazing, as he calmly asked the questions from the Ten Commandments.

He was even able to challenge them when they said they hadn't stolen anything by stating that he didn't believe them as they just told him they had admitted they had lied. You should have seen them laugh at that and then as happens almost all the time, they admitted to stealing something small when they were little.

Well, I could go on but you probably wouldn't read all of it. I pray that the comment below will impact you in your life as being a true statement for you.

"We are nobodies who can share with everybody about somebody who can save anybody"

Reflecting on What Happened at
The Maricopa County Jail December 2013

*J*ust got out of jail a while ago. Home now and reflecting on what happened.

Got there around 8:30AM and it took a while to get checked in. This was the first time that Nathan and Bob I came along with Midge and I to the what is called a "POD". This is where the inmates are held and can request a meeting with Christians who have been approved by the county to visit with them. The POD is a small room where a group of about fifteen or so inmates can come together to listen to some Bible readings and ask questions.

Bob brought his mandolin and Nathan brought his guitar. We all sang Christmas songs with the inmates and then Midge shared a story with them. We were blessed to be able to do these three separate times. We are also supposed to do two Chapel messages. This is where the inmates are escorted out of their cells from different sections in handcuffs to do the same thing. But there was a problem with one section of the prison and the inmates were not allowed out of their cells because the code word, "Lock-Down!!!".

I open in prayer, by taking a few deep breaths and asking for guidance from the Lord. I gave them what came to me. This is what I said to them. They were all here for a reason, and they understood why. They should realize that man's law had to be satisfied and if they were found guilty, they would have to do the time. The good news was that that sentence was temporary, as once their sentence was served, they would be set free. But they would still have to face a Holy, Righteous and Just God, and that would be the day when they die, and His Judgment would be eternal…either Heaven or Hell. (Hebrews 9:27)

With this in mind I then asked that the Lord would break their hearts, so that they would realize that they rightly deserved to be sent to Hell for disobeying God's Holy Laws, and at the same time have them REPENT and place their TRUST in the only one who could pay the fine for their crimes… Jesus the Christ. (1st Corinthians. 7:10)

Those that heard the message from all the PODS and the Chapel, clamored to receive the Million Dollar Gospel Tracts, as well as the Tract that asks "Which Religion is Right", and the Texting Tract.

They now have heard the Truth of what is required of those of us who are Law breakers. Riding home, Nathan mentioned how he saw many of their faces change after hearing it. Let us all pray that the Lord answers our prayers and tonight the Holy Spirit convicts them so that others may be adopted into the Kingdom of Heaven. (Ephesians1:5)

Me at Cigna Out-Patient January 2014

I wouldn't be sending this out except after what happened this morning at the hospital when I had my invasive procedure, which I rather not mention.

The doctor who performed my cancer surgery five years ago walks up to my bed and said, "So, Tom, how's life treating you?" I said I was blessed, how about you? He replied things were good. Then he asked an amazing question! So, Tom do you still have those Million Dollar Bills? I'm in the hospital bed, totally naked just a smock, and of course I had about 20 Million Dollar Gospel Tracts tucked under me. To say the least, I was shocked!

Here it is five years later this man that did my surgery still remembered it. I asked if he had read the back, he stated he did and it was convicting, as he still has it in his office. He's a surgeon! I say maybe he works 40 weeks of the year, takes some nice vacation time, and if he works five days a week in five years that's 1000 days that he's been with patients and for him to remember some old guy like me, well that's truly a gift from God.

Please, Please, people listen to this! I pray that you see this as an opportunity for those of us who claim Christ as the Lord of our life and change your mind about handing out the Word of God… these Million Dollar Gospel Tracts. They make an impact to those whom we meet no matter where… even a hospital.

As the staff gathered around me before they put me to sleep, I was able to give each one a Million-Dollar Gospel Tract and thanked them for being gentle with me right before this necessary invasive helpful surgery.

When I woke up a nurse, Mellissa was helping me get ready to leave. That's when I offered her one and told her that the back was going to ask if she was good enough to get into Heaven? She said yes! I then asked if I could ask her a few questions to see if that were true using some of God's

Ten Commandments. She said sure. When she admitted to breaking four of them, she still said that God would find her innocent, because God is a loving God. Well that's when she needed to hear the courtroom story, and when she heard it, she changed her mind.

Because I was still groggy, she helped me to the restroom and walked me in and as saw the mirror over the sink I turned to her and told her to look in the mirror. I told her that keeping the Ten Commandments wasn't going to save her, as no one has, but that mirror should show her how filthy dirty she is as well all of us are, and this is how God sees us nothing more than filthy rags. (Isaiah 64:6).

The only way we can become Born Again, righteous, saved, is to REPENT of all our sins and place our TRUST in Jesus Christ ALONE! For it was His death on the cross in Cavalry that paid the fine for all the crimes that we have committed. That's when she turned and looked directly at me and stated, "I need to thank you for sharing this, because of all the years I've been in Church, I've never heard it explained like that before, thank you!"

Now, here's my point! If it weren't for that Million Dollar Gospel Tract how would you be able to open a serious conversation about their eternal lives to a perfect stranger?

(Oh, I know just tell them Jesus Loves them)

Please read (1st Corinthians 1:18), to find out why you shouldn't.

This Night was Carter's Night

This Saturday was another blessing from the Lord!

Linda, who has been to a few of the seminar's asked me during the week if I was going out on Saturday night to Tempe. I also got a request from Rachel, and she comes all the way from Gilbert to meet us in Tempe, even though it was raining! It's heartwarming to see how this Biblical principle, using the, "Ten Commandments", to share is catching on to more and more of the Saints. Alan, and of course my loving wife Catherine, Dan, Marcus, as well as Matt and Mark were there as well.

They are now seeing the benefits of ASKING questions, about how they have broken the specific Commandments are more likely to listen to them and more importantly understand why they need a Savior, instead of TELLING those they speak to that they just need JESUS.

It's clear, the Scripture tells us!

"For the preaching of the cross is to them that perish foolishness; but unto us which are saved it is the power of God.

(1st Corinthians 1:18) KJV

It's truly amazing that even on this rainy night we can draw a crowd just because we offer money for answering trivia questions. Now that we have their attention, it's very easy to ask them a few questions to take the, " Good Person Test. "

One example was a young man named, Carter. He was one of several who stopped to take the Good Person Test, but in his case, there was conviction. He understood that what he was doing was offensive to a Holy God and he himself admitted that he would be punished and sent to Hell because of what he was doing.

This is the time when the Lord has prepared his heart to totally understand that there would be nothing, he could do to prevent God rightly sending him to Hell. The look on his face when he understood that was refreshing, as now he was ready to hear and understand what our Lord Jesus Christ did for me and now him on that Cross.

He now understood that just turning away from his sin wouldn't be enough. Jesus stated Himself unless you REPENT you will perish. (Luke13:3-5)

For the sorrow that is according to the will of God produces a repentance without regret, leading to salvation, but the sorrow of the world produces death. (2nd Corinthians 7:10) (NASB)

I also gave him Ephesians 2:8, 9, that it was only by the Grace of God that he was in front of me hearing this message. If he would repent and place his trust in Jesus Christ ALONE for the forgiveness of his sins, God would wipe the slate clean, he'd be free, and be an adopted child into the Kingdom of Heaven! Having predestined us unto the adoption of children by Jesus Christ to Himself, according to the kind intention of His will, (Ephesians 1:5) (KJV)

So please pray for Carter as he was a happy camper when he first came by me to collect his money for having the correct answer to the trivia questions, but as he was leaving his head was bowed down as he now was pondering his destiny for his future, as the Lord had shown him his sinful nature and prayerfully tonight he would become ,

"BORN AGAIN!"

A Tennis Match with Naphtali

Well this was the first tennis match beginning of 2014 with Naphtali and I.

Now that I'm 70 and he is 57, he assured me that he was going to win! Well today it didn't happened. We played for almost 90 minutes and I came out on top! 6-3 / 7-5.

Since we have been at this for about 8 or 9 yrs., and him being a devote Mormon, tried several times in the beginning to convert me, but no longer wanted to discuss in the later yrs. When I would quote him a Bible verse and ask him what it meant to him, he would always give me the same answer. It wasn't for him to answer, he stated, "I needed to "HUMBLE" myself and pray that the Lord through the Holy Spirit would reveal the Truth to me".

That's when I would ask again if he could just answer my question, but as always, he would repeat the same statement. Being I was asking him about our salvation as Jesus Himself, stated in John 3:3, "Being Born Again." Him not believing in that is probably the reason he made the excuse that I needed to ask the Holy Spirit about it.

The reason I can state how he responded was when we first started playing tennis, he would try to convince me that in order to get into Heaven I had to become a Mormon. That could only happen if I went with him to the Mormon Temple in Mesa, and have a Mormon Elder lay his hands on me. Also, just like Joseph Smith, I could become a god of my own planet.

After the match, I thanked him for sharing that with me and explained that the Lord had answered that question for me on Easter in 1994, as that was when I was Born again! That Jesus is the Only Begotten Son from God and He is NOT the brother of Satan nor did Jesus have any other brothers born of God, nor will any man become a God. Also, the statement that the Mormon Priesthood is the only authority God recognizes and is necessary for salvation is FALSE. Becoming a religion can't save you from going to HELL!

The only requirement to have eternal life in Heaven is to REPENT and Trust that His death on the Cross paid the fine for my Crimes. I also need to pray for anyone who believes differently.

His answer given to me AGAIN, was the same,

"humble yourself" **SAD!**

A Homeless Man with a Heart for God

May 2014

This Saturday night in Tempe, I decided to try to reach the lost from a different spot as the police gave me a difficult time last Saturday about being in front of the Post Office.

They told me I was not allowed to post my sign or even stand there, as it was tantamount to loitering. While they were reading me the riot act, I noticed a man alongside of me who you might guess was homeless.

After they left and as I was packing up, he stated that he loved what I was saying as he had heard me many times and wished he had said something to the officers about why they needed to hear what I was saying. Just before I left, he said wait a minute and started to write on what looked like a piece of paper that he took out of his backpack. He handed it to me; it was a Christmas card on which he wrote, "You're a blessed and highly favored Son of God, Thanks!

(Psalms 68:17, Malachi 3:1)

I don't know if you can imagine how I felt after this man did what he did. What a true blessing from the Lord! After being falsely accused the Lord sends me a messenger. This Saturday I set up by the movie theater across the street with my fellow sowers, Keith and Steve and started asking the question "Does anyone want a FREE Glow-Stick, just prove to me you're a good person!"

As I looked up there sitting on the curb was the same man who gave me the Christmas card. I waved to him and he gave me a big smile. A young lady and her male friend wanted to take the test, as she wanted her bulldog to have it. He was panting a lot, as it was a hot night. After taking the test and failing my brother in Christ Keith, asked me did I notice what the man who was sitting on his backpack by the curb did? I said no as I was concentrating on the two in front of me. He told me that he saw him get up and leave and when he came back, he had a Styrofoam cup in his hand. He then opened this backpack and took out a bottle of water and filled up the cup and them laid it alongside of the dog.

Later that night when we were leaving, he came over to us and thanked me for speaking to all those who stopped to take the test and then asked if we had $0.55, so he could get a refill for his coffee. I was able to give him a dollar and when Keith and Steve tried to give him what they had he wouldn't take it as he restated that he only needed $0.55 for his coffee.

I don't know about you but I haven't seen that kind of generosity or humility from anyone in his situation. He differently reminded me of the good Samaritan.

Inmate's 8-year-old daughter prays for Dad

She tells her Dad she is praying that God would send someone to speak to him July 2014

On Monday July 7th, three of us went to Maricopa County Jail.

Midge, she's about 85 years old, Catherine and myself. We usually arrive around 8:30AM. This Monday was truly a blessing for them and us, as we were able to see more inmates than usual. Usually we leave the jail around 2 to 2:30PM, but this Monday we didn't leave till 4 o'clock.

In our 2nd session, one of the young men in his early twenty's, stated several times, "it doesn't make sense!" He had heard many times about Jesus dying on the cross to pay for our sins, again he states, "doesn't make sense!"

That's when I walked over and sat down next to him and asked him what doesn't make sense? He stated, "If someone who lives his life and breaks every single one of God's Laws and then right before he dies on his deathbed, he accepts Jesus, are you telling me that that person is going to heaven? That doesn't make sense!" I've been told many times that Jesus loves me and all I have to do is accept Him and I'm saved, so I might as well get what I can and before I die, then I'll ask em.

That's when I shared with him what I learned from Ray Comfort who brought us the teaching of The Way of The Master. I then asked him if he had ever lied, stolen or used the Lord's Name as a swear word, or ever looked with lust? He stated he had, with a flippant attitude!

I then asked, based on his own admission, would he be innocent or guilty in front of a Holy God...He said guilty! I then asked Heaven or Hell, he stated Hell. I then asked did that concern him he said, "NO!" I then explained what Hell is like. I have found that many even those who claim to be Christian don't really know.

He now changed his tune bout being concerned about spending eternity there. Now as you can see, his understanding of a god who will just set you free because you accept him, didn't make sense and rightly so.

Here is where I was able to give him the courtroom analogy that Ray had shown us. If he was in front of the Maricopa Judge and was about to be sentenced with the Judge stating he would have to spend life in jail or come up with one million dollars, to be set free. I then asked so if he just told the Judge how sorry he was, please forgive me, and I'll never do it again, could the Judge let him go? He stated no!

I then asked what if just as the Judge was about to slam the gavel down for his sentence of life in prison, when someone he didn't know walked into the courtroom and shouted out that he had a certified check for $1 Million Dollars. The man states he sold everything he had, Stocks, Bonds, Investment property, cars and his house because he loves this man and didn't want to see him suffer.

I then asked the inmate could the Judge let you go? He pondered a while and then with a smile, said, "YES!" That's when I told him that's what Jesus did for us two thousand years ago. What is needed from us now, and in this case him, (the inmate) is NOT to just accept Jesus, but to REPENT, (have Godly sorrow) and TRUST in Him for the forgiveness of our sins, and if he does then I would assume that he would do as He requested,

"to go and sin NO MORE!"

Praise the Lord! It was a blessing as not only did his body language change, but he also stated, "Now I understand, that makes sense!"

I asked him to seriously think about what he has heard and when he goes back to his cell that he may want to get on his knees, no on his face, and ask the Lord to forgive him of all his sins, even name them, then share that experience with others in the jail.

Please pray for this young man as I think the Lord was calling him, as when I was finished talking, he made an amazing statement.

His eight-year-old daughter spoke with him last week and told him, that she was praying that God would send someone to speak to him.

Sharing the Gospel at Burger King on Bell Rd.

September 2014

Thursday David and I went to Burger King for a late lunch.

The man who took our order put a big smile on his face when I asked him if he could make change of the Million Dollar Gospel Tract. This question almost always has the same reaction, and think of it, not only do they smile but know he has the Word of God in his hand and by God's Grace, after he reads the back could as Paul says it, " be adopted into the Kingdom of Heaven." How great is that?

We took our seats and started to pray after a short while and as I finished the man was standing a few feet away from me with our order. He said he was sorry, as he hadn't realized that I was praying. That's when I shared with him if I knew he was there I would have asked him if it was okay if we prayed before we eat? That is what I do any time I am served a meal. I then told him what I always ask next...is there anything I can pray for you about? You should have seen the shocked look on his face...he then said "a better job! "

After David and I finished eating he was there again this time to take away our tray. That's when I showed him how the Commemorative Coin with God's Ten Commandments on one side and the Gospel of Jesus Christ on the other suddenly appears. That's when I explain what's on it and how sad it is that very few, even those who claim to be Christians know them!

I then shared the other tracts I carry like.

"Which Religion is Right", "Would you like to be Debt Free? "

I could see now that he was interested as he was thanking me each time I gave him one.

I then asked if his cell phone could print out a business card and showed him how mine did print it out of my phone and put in his hand. Now he was truly amazed as I told him that this card had a silver spot and if he were to hold his thumb there for 15 seconds, and if he was a good person it would turn GREEN. He tried and of course it didn't.

NOW COMES WHY I'M WRITING THIS....

He then asked me, "was I hiring?" I was shocked! Remember his prayer request? He now wanted to learn how to share with others the way I had shared with him. I told him of the teaching I do at our Church and told him to contact me from my website. **www.tillthenetsRFull.org** about it.

I then asked David why he thought Christians who see how this works, refuse to do it? He thought for a while, and then said they're cowards! I shared with him that maybe they should read (Revelations 21:8), as the word cowardly is the first in the list of all who will have their part in the lake of fire.

Please pray that our server does, as Jesus Himself prayed to our Heavenly Father, to send more laborers. (Luke 10:2)

Ever Asked, How Was Your Day? Here's Mine

I was blessed today by being asked by one of the ladies who attends our church, and can't drive, asked if I could take her to the doctor.

At the doctor's office, an elderly man came in wearing a jacket with Apollo patches all over it. A young man asked him if he was an Astronaut? He stated he wasn't but was at Cape Canaveral, and got the jacket there. He told the young man how impressed he was at what these Astronauts accomplished, that's why he wears the jacket. The young man shook his hand to congratulate him for wearing it.

As I was leaving, I told him that I thought the jacket was awesome and it was worth a Million. I gave him the Million Dollar Gospel Tract and he had a big smile and thanked me. I then said, the young man that appreciated you wearing that jacket when he comes out from the visit, do you think he would like one as well? With that another big smile and believe it or not he put out his hand and said sure!

From there the lady and I stopped at Denny's for a bite. We had been to this Denny's last month after her visit and we got the same waitress, Sierra. I asked if she remembered us? I remember her being pregnant. She said she didn't remember us. After we gave our order, I asked her if it would be okay with her as we pray before we eat? She said, "GO AHEAD!" Then I asked was there was anything I could pray for you about? That's when she got all excited and stated, "NOW I REMEMBER YOU!" She then placed her hand on my shoulder, and I offered her my hand as she requested that we pray for her baby girl to be healthy.

Later the General Manger came over and asked if everything was okay. I stated that I had a problem and he asked with what? I then showed him the Red and Blue Gospel Tract illusion on the table and asked him if he could tell me why they look different when they are the same size.

He was enamored, so I gave him the cards so he could read why it was like that. I also told him to show his EE's. He then told me about his family and that he had three children. That's when I asked him about their magical saltshaker and produced the Ten Commandment Coin.

He smiled at that and then asked what is it? I told him it was a Commemorative coin and it had the Ten Commandments on one side and the Gospel of Jesus Christ on the other. He liked that and because he had three children, I gave him two more. He was extremely appreciative as he told me no one had ever given him anything since he's worked there.

From there we went to Wal-Mart's to get her prescription, and do some food shopping. While walking around getting food, several people received Million Dollar Gospel Tracts, because they either bumped into me or because she uses a motorized cart and blocked what people were looking at.

While standing trying to decide what to get, few of them stared at what to buy, so I offered them one as well to help them decide. One special encounter was a man with his wife and daughter who was behind me in line to check out. I told him he could go first, and with a little coaching he did. That's when I offered him the Million Dollar Gospel Tract and he thanked me for letting them go first.

I told him it was a blessing for me because he and his family were worth a Million. As his wife was putting their items on the conveyor, he started to read the back. He gave me thumbs up and I told him that when he was driving home to have his daughter read it to them as well.

Now as we checked out, I asked the cashier if her cash register makes change and placed the Million Dollar Gospel Tract on the counter. She laughed and slid it by the register. I asked her to read the back when she was on her break as it is worth more the a Million. Praise the LORD for the printing press.

Now on the streets in Tempe offering free Glow-Sticks, I would like you to pray for Tyler. He stopped by around 11PM and was curious as to why I was given away Glow-Sticks. I found out that he was in summer school and wanted to get extra credits so that he could graduate sooner and was majoring in Physics. WOW! Physics! I never meet anybody majoring in Physics, nevertheless taking extra courses to graduate sooner.

Here was a young man, who my heart went out to, as he started to explain to me EVOLUTION...YUK! After his presentation I asked him where did the first entity come from that started it all? He then stated no one knows. That's when I asked how then can you claim your view as being SCIENCE, when you yourself can't prove it scientifically? Isn't that just an opinion?

Well now comes the best part as two other not so sober young men butted in and wanted a Glow-Stick. I walked them through the four questions about lying, stealing, blasphemy and lust. They all responded with yes answers including Tyler who still was in the middle of these two men.

One of the them didn't like what the outcome was to those who violate God's Law and stated he was going into Heaven no matter what he does as his F@#*ing mother is there to let him in, (What a disgusting thing for this young man to say) I had no choice but to reprimand him on that comment! He then pulled the other man away with him as he could see his friend was wanting to listen to me. Now alone again with Tyler I explained being his science was just another man's opinion. What if what the Bible states is true? I then gave him what (Job 26:7) states. "That the earth is hanging on nothing."

I mentioned that that was written about four thousand years ago and if man and or the Roman Catholic Church was reading the word of God, back in 1492, they would have given Christopher Columbus the boats he wanted to sail to a new world. Instead, telling him the world was flat and he would fall off.

If the Roman Catholic Church had truly understood the Bible, they wouldn't have put Galileo under house arrest just because he stated the world was round and revolved around the sun, NOT the other way around. In today's science he would be called an Astronomer, as he used a telescope. Science and this Roman Catholic man-made religion were wrong then but interesting no longer believe in the flat Earth theory.

I could see his demeanor starting to change. As he intently listened to what I was saying, and was no longer trying to validate his statements. That's when I gave him the GOOD news that Jesus Christ died for his and my sins.

He took the punishment that I deserved. If he truly understands this then what's needed on his part is to REPENT, (2nd Cor. 7:10) and place his TRUST in Jesus Christ ALONE for the forgiveness of his sins. NOT what we do but what He has done for us. (Ephesians 2:8,9)

He reached up and shook my hand and thanked me for taking the time to share with him. That's when I asked if he would read a Tract I use "Are you good enough to get to Heaven?" He took it and said he would. Please pray for Tyler that The Lord reveals the Truth to him and he is adopted into the Kingdom of Heaven!

At the Dentist Office 2015

Had to share this, I'm at the dentist's office this morning having some work done.

I was told I had to come back and they would call me. That's when I asked if they had my number and was holding my phone when I asked. One went to the computer to find out, the other took my money and receptionist was also looking at me then. That's when I asked do you use cell phones a lot?

I then asked can their cell phone print out a business card not using blue-tooth to a printer? All three stated. "NO WAY!" That's when I showed them the app called, "Tract Printer" and a card is audibly and visually displayed on the screen and because I have this card behind the phone you just have to slide it out and that's when you get to see the surprised look and gapping eyes on their faces and how wide they opened their mouths. This card has a silver square on it and asks, "if they place their thumb on it and count to fifteen, if it turns green, they are a good person".

This gave me the perfect opportunity to walk them through the, "Good Person Test". I asked had they ever lied, stolen, sworn, or looked with lust? All of them said they had. I then asked if God where to judge them how would He find them, innocent or guilty? They stated guilty and then I asked where would He have to send them, Heaven or Hell?

The reason I'm sharing this is to prayerfully you can see that even in a busy Dentist office using this simple Biblical principal that Jesus Himself used in Luke 18:18, can help those who may be lost who seem to have the impression that God who is love would never send anyone to Hell. Now I was able to share with them the Good News as to why Jesus had to die on the Cross to pay the penalty for all the sins we have committed.

The final point I needed to make was that now, hearing this for the first time, they need to REPENT and TRUST in Jesus Christ alone for the forgiveness of their sins. I explained how this can only happen by God's free gift. "By Grace we have been saved, it's a gift from God, not of works so that no one can boast." (Ephesians 2:8-9)

Finally, here's my question for you. Have you ever shared God's Law with anyone at their professional office? If you would like to know how to use this approach let me know.

My Radio Show, Can You Hear Me Now? 2018

*W*ell now it's April 2018 and I get a call from someone who knew me and had even attended one of my many seminars on how to reach the lost using Ray Comfort's Biblical principle of how to reach the lost.

He mentioned that after hearing what I teach and have been doing it for many years…well here it comes he stated that the world needs to hear this message and how would I like to have my own Internet Radio Show. Well how would you respond to such a request? I was in shock, but the Lord being present with me gave me the courage to respond with YES, what would I have to do?

He then explained I would be able to make my presentation for 30 minutes and it would air on Wednesday starting at 7PM and continue to repeat every half hour until 10 PM. He then stated that it would also air again on Sunday nights for 30 minutes starting at 8PM.

My responsibility would be every Tuesday night to call in with what I wanted to say and it would be recorded and then played as he stated earlier.

So, starting on May 1st I made my first presentation for my 30-minute Internet Radio Show. Oh, here comes the unexpected, he also asked me what I would like to call my radio show? What the Lord gave me as my response was.

"Can You Hear Me Now?"

I would then follow that up when

I was broadcasting the show with,

"Can You Hear Me Now?" … "Are you Listening?"

My first recording was about my transformation from being misled by the Roman Catholic religion to now being a Born-Again believer in Jesus the Christ for my Salvation.

Here's what the topic was called:

I WAS… I AM NOW… and I SHALL EVER BE!

To my surprise the number of listeners over the eight-month period, grew exponentially!

This was truly a blessing from the Lord!

If you would like, you can read or listen to the thirty-two 30-minute shows I did then. http://bit.ly/2mDNgEh

Sadly, after eight months of recording this show every week, the producer told me my show was being canceled.

Our 23rd Wedding Anniversary

June 17th 2018

Well, how's this for celebrating our 23rd Anniversary and giving thanks to the Lord for bringing us together.

I pray you will see how easy these Million Dollar Gospel Tracts are to share with strangers, but you will have to carry them with you at all times, as you'll never know when you'll need them. Look how these four strangers who were sitting at two separate tables near us got excited after receiving these unique Gospel Tracts, with the Word of God on them.

Catherine and I went to Carlos O'Brien to celebrate our Twenty-Third anniversary. I started to share with Catherine about a lengthy email I received from a friend of ours, Patricia. It was about God being the creator and the SIN defect appeared in mankind through Adam and Eve and continued in all mankind. Humans needed to contact Jesus as He was willing to bear the cost of bringing them back to Him.

I then shared what I was going to use on my Radio Show on Wednesday night, "Can You Hear Me Now" about a famous quote from the Prince of Preachers Charles Spurgeon. I was asking why is it that all the churches we've attended refuse to elevate God's Law as a primary reason to help the lost understand why they need Jesus.

I also gave the quote from Paul in 1st Corinthians 1:18, that literally says: "For the preaching of the cross is foolishness to those who are perishing, but to us who are being saved it is the power of God." If it is foolishness to speak about Jesus 1st, then using the Law 1st makes sense.

And here's what Spurgeon stated:

"I do not believe that any man can preach the gospel who does not preach Law. The Law is the needle, and you cannot draw the silken thread of the gospel through a man's heart until you first send the Law to make way for it. If men do not understand the Law, they will not feel they are sinners and if they are not conscious sinners, they will never value the sin offering. There is no healing a man until the Law has wounded him, no making him alive until the Law has slain him."

Well, here it comes! an elderly man sitting behind Catherine shouted how he loved Jesus and raised his hand and gave me a thumb up! We were just about ready to leave so, I got up and handed him a Million Dollar Gospel Tract for acknowledging what I was sharing with Catherine. With that, he had a big smile and then stated, "that this is my daughter, who's celebrating Father's Day with me."

With that, I gave her one as well for being a loving daughter. Because of him telling me how much he loved Jesus, I shared with her how her silver spoon was amazing as I now snapped my fingers twice and the Ten Commandments Coin appeared out from the spoon. You should have seen the look on her face. I explained to her that it was a Commemorative coin and had the Ten Commandments on one side and the Gospel of Jesus the Christ on the other. I then stated how sad it is today that there is so little teaching about them, and one day we might be judged by them.

Just then I heard a man at next table saying out loud, "hey can I have one those coins?" Now, standing next to him he's telling me he is with his daughter. I thanked him for asking for the coin by giving him a Million Dollar Gospel Tract. Being his daughter had her back to where I was before I then showed her the magic from the top of a salt shaker next to her and with two snaps of my finger, the Ten Commandments Coin appears.

You should have seen her reaction as she bent backward and placed both of her hands over her face. With that the Father thanked me, so I gave him a coin and told them to read the back of the bill because it's worth more than a Million and if you go to the web site, you'll get a free gift. He put out his hand and thanked me.

So, tell me if our conversation wasn't about the Lord and if I didn't have these unique tracts to hand out, our time would have been just like another day eating out and not sharing the wonderful gift the Lord gave to Catherine and I and selfishly be like most who are only concerned about themselves.

Now it's time to say AMEN!

I'd like to finish with a humble thankyou to the Lord for revealing Himself to me at the time He destined for me to know Him.

I pray that anyone who reads this book and has not truly been Born Again, that with what Paul states in 2nd Corinthians 7:10, helps.

"For the sorrow that is according to the will of God produces a repentance without regret, leading to salvation, but the sorrow of the world produces death." (NASB)

Then in (2nd Corinthians 5:17)

"Therefore, if anyone is in Christ, he is a new creature; the old things passed away; behold, new things have come." (NASB)

With that in mind I pray you are one who now will trust and obey the Lord on what He requires from those of us whom He has called, to go out of your way to share with anyone who crosses your path.

Appendix: Links them

My Webpage http://www.tillthenetsrfull.org/

2008

Japan Mission Trip - January 2008 https://bit.ly/2lFc4ez

2009

One of the Exciting Moments August https://bit.ly/2lYaZi3

Way of the Master October https://bit.ly/2ka8lW8

Just another lunch at Mongolian Barbecue http://bit.ly/2lUf07g

2010

God's Saturday Blessing at Pat's Pizza January https://bit.ly/2kpcgyv

Navajo Indian taking the Good Person Test at McDonalds February https://bit.ly/2lJT1zF

Honoring the Lord Today July for the Glory to God at McDonald's https://bit.ly/2kpcaa7

Way of the Master Seminar July https://bit.ly/2lEkOSl

Husband and Wife taking the Good Person Test August https://bit.ly/2knQo6F

Stone Age or New Technology September https://bit.ly/2m0G9W4

Is it TRUE that you just need to BELIEVE? September https://bit.ly/2kpcRAf

Reaching out to the lost in Tempe AZ September https://bit.ly/2k30468

1st Friday Night at the Phoenix Art Fair October https://bit.ly/2lZAO1b

Wednesday Morning at McDonalds October https://bit.ly/2lJfn4h

Saturday Night in Tempe w/Tree of Life Church October https://bit.ly/2k30mde

It's NOT a secret ANYMORE! The Phoenix Magazine https://bit.ly/2kxm9dn

Our Seed Sower Team in Tempe Saturday November https://bit.ly/2lAklQZ

Sharing Jesus Christ on ASU Campus November https://bit.ly/2kpdrOr

1st Friday Night on the streets in Phoenix November https://bit.ly/2lZAWOd

Singing Hallelujah Chorus at Scottsdale Fashion Square Scottsdale AZ December https://bit.ly/2kA69Ho

Eleven Comments about this post from my Blog https://bit.ly/2lBQYhk

2011

A Cold Saturday Night in Tempe On Mill Ave. https://bit.ly/2m5tmBS

Way of the Master and Beyond January https://bit.ly/2m2EY8B

A Night to Glorify the Lord Jesus The Christ January https://bit.ly/2lBRHiy

Our New Banner Asking ARE YOU A GOOD PERSON February https://bit.ly/2m4iPH8

1st Friday Night at 3rd and *Roosevelt Phoenix February* https://bit.ly/2kA8Rg3

Saturday Night with Catherine March https://bit.ly/2kxwaHt

Saturday Night in Tempe then Taco Bell April https://bit.ly/2kye9sA

Some Comments from the Way of The Master Seminar May https://bit.ly/2kA6TMG

Let, "YOUR LIGHT SHINE" https://bit.ly/2klby5j

You're going to LOVE this! July https://bit.ly/2kA99DF

1st Friday at Phoenix Art Fair **August** https://bit.ly/2m2FfZb

Saturday Night on Mill in Tempe August https://bit.ly/2m2FkvX

Spenser Taking the Good Person Test September https://bit.ly/2m4jh8i

Prayer Alone??? September https://bit.ly/2lCSRu2

September at the 1st Friday at the Art Fair https://bit.ly/2lJylru

Saturday Night on Mill Ave Tempe November https://bit.ly/2Zy2koL

Please Pray for Amanda November https://bit.ly/2lI1fZ4

Jacob Takes off his Rosary Beards December https://bit.ly/2m4jto2

Prayers as Junior hears the WHOLE TRUTH December https://bit.ly/2lJSspx

Way of the Master Seminar with NEW Sowers https://bit.ly/2kyWyRk

2013

Thomas Fusco Post from my Blog June https://bit.ly/2kyeN9u

2014

What Happened to Me at Cigna Out-Patient January https://bit.ly/2kpeJJh

A Homeless Man with a Heart for God May https://bit.ly/2lAlojT

Inmate's 8-year-old daughter prays for Dad July https://bit.ly/2lCbsGI